GLIMPSES OF ANOTHER LAND

Glimpses of Another Land

Political Hopes, Spiritual Longing

Essays

Eric Miller

CASCADE *Books* · Eugene, Oregon

GLIMPSES OF ANOTHER LAND
Political Hopes, Spiritual Longing: Essays

Cascade Books
An Imprint of Wipf and Stock Publishers
199 W. 8th Ave., Suite 3
Eugene, OR 97401

www.wipfandstock.com

ISBN 13: 978-1-61097-835-4

Cataloging-in-Publication data:

Miller, Eric.

   Glimpses of another land : political hopes, spiritual longing: essays / Eric Miller.

   x + 180 p. ; 23 cm.

   ISBN 13: 978-1-61097-835-4

   1. Hope—Religious aspects. 2. Hope—Social aspects—United States. 3. Spiritual life—United States. I. Title. II. Series

BD216 M50 2012

Manufactured in the U.S.A.

For Kathleen Ann and William Bradley Miller

Radicals

For Betty Jane and Wenten Riley Miller[†]

Agrarians

Contents

Contents

SPORT

FAITH

Acknowledgments

INSPIRATION CAN COME FROM anywhere. But completion requires a rare—indeed, inspired!—form of aid. For providing both I am indebted to many fine editors, including Katelyn Beatty, Mark Galli, Josh Gohlke, Stan Guthrie, Richard Kauffman, Tom Kennedy, Bob Kruschwitz, Doug LeBlanc, Damon Linker, Michael Maudlin, David Mills, David Neff, James Nuechterlein, Ted Olsen, Caleb Stegall, Sarah Koops Vanderveen, and John Wilson.

The collecting and revising of these essays was made possible by the generous support of the Louise S. Walker History Endowment at Geneva College, as well as the college's faculty development program. Special thanks to William, Susan, and Lucas Kriner.

Wipf and Stock's support for this book has, from beginning to end, been heartening. My thanks especially to Chris Spinks for his editorial efforts and Kristen Bareman for her superb work in design.

I believe in a gracious and immanent God for many reasons. Central among these is the presence of Robert Strauch in Cuiabá, Brazil between 1980 and 1982. As a teacher and friend, he intervened in the life of a very confused teenager in decisive ways, among which were his requirement that I write often and his encouragement of me when I did. He made me write essays. He made me write about what matters. Gratitude wells from deep, deep within.

Since 2003 I have had the honor of participating in a team-taught course called Invitation to the Humanities (or in Genevaspeak, "HUM 103"). It has been a revolutionary experience, one propelled by companionship with as merry a band as a fellow could hope for. For inspiration, camaraderie, comedy, and vision, I thank all of the past and present members of the team, but especially Robert Frazier and Shirley

Acknowledgments

Kilpatrick. The mind and spirit of HUM 103 are present throughout this book.

Suhail Hanna has for many years been a true companion in the writing life. It is a joy to share this road with him.

Denise, my wife, listened to ideas, endured the writing days (and nights), offered cogent commentary, and, as ever, provided good cheer. My writing springs from a place I share gratefully with her. Our sons, Ian, Luke, and Kit, have provided inspiration and motivation I will never be able fully to trace. Their hilarity, wit, and hope keep me attuned to the world that is actually before me.

I've dedicated this book to my parents and to my father's parents. In the midst of flux and fluidity of remarkable dimensions, they have with evident integrity stood for a way of seeing and living that reveals the promise of life. As I hope they'll see as they read these pages, I am their grateful son.

Introduction

Political Hope, Spiritual Longing

OF ALL THE DISTINCTIVE raiment with which Americans garb themselves, political hope is surely the most evident to anyone not American.
We put it on without thinking. We seldom take it off. We have varieties
for all weather. It is so natural to us we sense its absence as nakedness,
disturbing degradation. We Americans are not defined by particular
cultural practices or a distinctive landscape so much as by this insistent,
encompassing hope.

As hope, ours is not always very impressive, which is to say it's often specious. But its durability is remarkable. I was raised in an American Protestant tradition that has at its core an apocalyptic eschatology
proclaiming the certain, imminent collapse of human civilization as we
know it. In Sunday school classes, in sermons, and at what were called
"prophecy conferences" we heard grand and awful pronouncements of
an End that was already arriving. The child of missionaries, I recall as
a teenager in the middle of South America listening to a recorded sermon by Hal Lindsey called "The 1980s: Countdown to Armageddon."
After hearing it at home I was impelled to take it to our little American
school so the teacher could play it in Bible class. He did.[1] This end-
times, time-is-ending narrative suffused our thinking about the world.
About everything.

Everything except the United States. Here, amazingly, hope, despite the encroaching desolation, pounded its rhythm deep into the
night. Some managed to preserve hope for America by locating in
Scripture an exception clause for the United States amidst civilization's

1. But did he agree with it? I don't know. He was a very courteous and generous man.

1

demise. But for most this native political hope was less self-conscious, less cerebral, and more instinctual. In America there is always the possibility that we can get things right, make things new. What else could *America* mean?

It's no surprise at all, then, that as Hal Lindsey in the 1970s and 1980s was convincing millions of Americans that the end of the age was coming, many of those same Americans were lining up at the polls and at abortion rallies to "save the culture." They were Christians. But they were American Christians. Which identity is more decisive? It is never easy to tell.

Hope being a theological virtue, it's tricky to mount an argument against it. And perhaps that, in the end, is why American hope has steadily won out against more dour eschatologies (and clearly Protestant premillennialism is only one among many) that would stimulate other forms of response. We *should* hope: this we know.

This book is American in many ways, but perhaps most distinctively in its hopefulness. At the same time, it reflects an effort to be fundamentally and thoroughly Christian. This pairing of identities is, I'm suggesting, fraught. Christians know that not just any hope will do, whether American or any other kind. Hope is required of us but so is intelligence; our theology, in fact, insists that these belong together, that the absence of hope dims the intellect, that the absence of mind diminishes the virtue. Christian hoping must emerge from our deepest understanding of reality, our truest apprehension of being and time. And it must call into question and subordinate all other visions and intuitions of what is, and what is to come.

If Americans are born with the birthright of hope, the challenge for American Christians is to shape, hone, and direct it in such a way as to yield a smart, wise, and fruitful politics, a politics that seeks to make evident in any given sphere the unspeakable reality of God. Understood in this way, politics—whether on the scale of the nation, the township, the church, or the home—is simply the working out in our daily life of our deepest beliefs. It is the register of our fundamental moral impulses and intelligence. It is the evidence of what we think, of how we think, of whether we think. We are indeed political animals, as Aristotle averred. And nothing better shows how we understand the meaning of our circumstance and moment than the ways in which we as communities frame, order, and establish our lives together. We face no greater challenge than the challenge of politics. And maintaining intelligent political hope is the truest test we know of our character, mind, and vision.

The essays that follow are above all the fruit of a long, ongoing quest for this hopeful intelligence; it is indeed this questing that makes them essays in the first place. For me, the hoping has come easily enough; where to go with it has been the larger challenge. As I was listening to Hal Lindsey as a teenager in the early 1980s I was watching Ronald Reagan. The first term paper I wrote as a high-schooler in that little school for the children of missionaries was a biography of Alexander Haig, Reagan's first Secretary of State. My friend Richie, another nascent political animal whose parents were Baptist missionaries from Kentucky, stoked my Young Republican enthusiasms; we recovered from the humiliation of the Nixon and Carter years by flaunting our American identity in a foreign land, cheering on the proud, kindly, confident leader whose enormous shadow covered Brazil and beyond. Preparing as a college freshman a little while later to cast my first vote, I witnessed Reagan in person at a rally just before the election and cheered until my lungs gave out. The cheering came from deep within.

But by 1992, eight years later, much was changing within me, catalyzed by the abrupt end of the Reagan years with the election of Bill Clinton and emerging from a surge toward spiritual and intellectual maturity that had begun a few years earlier. I was no longer a child, I knew; childish thinking—childish hoping—I had to push aside. A quest for a new politics, for a mature politics, was beginning. This is what deepening faith seemed to require: a set of convictions about what our common life, at all levels, should look like.

This book is a testament of this quest, affording glimpses of growth (I hope), struggle (I know), and at times (who's to say?) vision. The social criticism herein is deeply enmeshed in personal odyssey—yet it is an odyssey that is, I believe, not simply personal. This story is not simply my own, as the stories of others have helped me to see.

The essays span a decade of crisis, from the disputed Gore-Bush election of 2000, through the shock of September 11, 2001 and the wars that have followed, to the economic meltdown of 2008 and our subsequent malaise. And this, of course, is just to mark time by the most obvious political events. The deeper dynamics of the decade, whether ecological, moral, or intellectual, reveal a vast multidimensional fracturing no amount of microfiber can mend. It's this deeper historical moment that these essays above all seek to confront, and my focus is predominantly on it rather than on, for instance, federal policy or national politics. I've divided the essays into thematic sections: earth, politics, education, sport, and faith. But this is just a convenience. The thinking runs together; the vision is whole, or is an effort in that direction. The parts are parts, not apart.

This perception of fracture and longing for wholeness tips my hand and reveals, too, the play of generational change. In the fall of 2000, in my second year as a professor at Geneva College, I was teaching a course in the history of political thought. Early in the semester we read a 1999 *Atlantic Monthly* essay titled "A Politics for Generation X," by Ted Halstead. Having, as usual, assigned it without having read it, I was especially delighted to find myself nodding vigorously throughout. At some point it occurred to me that all of my nodding was a sign of autobiographical discovery: the political journey I had been on was more of a collective pilgrimage than I had to that point been able to see. "America," noted Halstead, "has some of the worst rates of child poverty, infant mortality, teen suicide, crime, family breakup, homelessness, and functional illiteracy in the developed world . . . many of our cities have turned into islands of despair, a frightening number of our public schools are dangerous, and almost two million of our residents are behind bars." His conclusion was understated and, to me, quite evident: "Many Xers sense that the basic fabric of American society is somehow fraying."

Halstead went on to describe the politics he saw emerging in my generational cohort as anchored by a "constellation of beliefs" that "transcends the existing left-right spectrum." It included "Fiscal prudence, economic populism, social investment, campaign reform, shared sacrifice, and environmental conservation." But what I had been feeling most acutely he articulated in his next line: "It should be immediately apparent that this generation's voice is not represented by any of the established leaders or factions in the political mainstream."

Indeed, what I had in those years been discovering was precisely the vital presence of leaders and voices beyond this mainstream, emerging from a complex and unfamiliar past, whose work promised illumination—and thus hope. Those who know the terrain will recognize, even anticipate, the influences—Wendell Berry, G. K. Chesterton, and Alasdair MacIntyre, among others. One of these influences in particular requires a further word. During the time most of these essays were written I was also working on a PhD dissertation on the American historian and social critic Christopher Lasch, which I eventually turned into a book. I had discovered Lasch shortly after the disorienting Clinton triumph, and after reading Lasch's remarkable volume *The True and Only Heaven: Progress and Its Critics*, then just recently published, I found myself on the trail he was making, having, I now see, no idea at all how far it would take me or even where it would lead. Much of the thinking that shaped my biography of Lasch, *Hope in a Scattering Time* (2010), was worked out in these essays; many of Lasch's ideas, and I suppose more generally his stance, have in turn molded me in ways I can hardly see, much less describe.

More than ten years after Halstead's manifesto appeared, I'm not sure of the extent to which his predictions have held up. What I do know is that the problems he identified are ones that many in my generation, as well as many on either side of it, have felt deeply, and have experienced as an aching presence pervading all that we do, whether at church, at school, in the neighborhood, on the job, or in the home. For engaging this world and bringing healing to it, the politics of "left" and "right" are blunt instruments indeed. The judgment with which Lasch in 1991 began *The True and Only Heaven* has if anything more force today than it did two decades past: the "old political ideologies have exhausted their capacity either to explain events or to inspire men and women to constructive action." In the face of our dark and difficult moment, these essays, many of them written in a confessional vein, are simply an effort to find light and to give it—the kind of light that, invariably, keeps hope alive.

Prologue

Keeping Up with the Amish

WE LIVE AMIDST THE Amish.[1] Tractors now seem strange to us, and slightly profane; teams of horses plow our fields. No longer does a horse and buggy at an ATM rate more than a passing glance, and it only seems right that shopping centers have hitching posts. Here the mighty beasts of the landscape are made not of steel but flesh and blood. Modern farm gadgetry is just a rumor.

Today I took my customary Amishland run. A few times a week I trot twice around a two-mile loop, a course that takes me through or alongside four Amish farms and several other Amish homes connected to these farms. When we first moved here two years ago I ventured out with a sense of caution, and some trepidation. Not only do a variety of automobiles race along these narrow roads, but horse-propelled buggies do too. *What is the proper approach to a horse and buggy?* This was a question I'd never seen addressed in running magazines. Does one cross to the other side to avoid being chased or chomped? Can these bearded drivers be trusted to keep carriage and horse on course? Closer to the heart, would the Amish sneer at an *Englisher* (their name for us) jogging on their roads, alongside their farms? "Why does that man run, Papa?," I imagined a child asking his father. "Because," replies the sage, "even their bodies demand work of some kind. You can't sit around all day and expect rest for the soul at night."

1. When I wrote this essay my family lived in Lancaster County, Pennsylvania, just a mile or so from the Nickel Mines school that would become the center of national attention in the fall of 2006 when a man shot and killed five girls there and wounded many others. This essay was awarded second place in *Christianity Today's* 1998 Faith and Consumerism writing contest.

My fears were in vain. Horses generally do avoid runners, and the Amish wave politely as we cross paths, sometimes calling out a greeting. I've detected nothing more hostile than perhaps a muffled snicker. Three times today I passed a middle-aged Amish woman and a young girl walking the opposite way around the loop, apparently out for exercise as well. At our first encounter we exchanged hellos. At the second, about ten minutes later, the woman caught me off guard, shouting, "You make us look sick!" "Yeah," I yelled back, "but I *feel* sick!" At our third meeting she called out, with a hardy Pennsylvania Dutch accent, "Don't tell me you've done the whole loop again!" I merely nodded, now incapable of vocal exertion. "Give me a year," she retorted. My spirits were buoyed by the exchange. Decent, peaceable, kind: the Amish, or "the still in the land," as they were once known, are fine neighbors, even to those of us who indulge in such odd practices as jogging, peculiar folkway of post-industrial America.

As I run I often find myself trying to gauge how the Amish are faring in their battle to keep the modern world at bay and their own way of life intact. This day, as some children bob by on their way to their little school house, a visual incongruence jars me: amidst the collage of blacks, blues, purples, and browns I see *neon pink*. Thermoses, it seems, have made it on to their back-to-school lists. Is this a bad sign? Donald B. Kraybill and Steven M. Nolt, in their study *Amish Enterprise: From Plows to Profits*, warn that the market economy is indeed making inroads even among the Amish; business concerns play an increasingly dominant role in a sizable number of families. Apparently this is discomfiting to many within their community. Kraybill and Nolt record the cryptic counsel of one Amish woman: "You shouldn't be in business if you are married." Is she a crotchety member of a generation about to be passed by or a prescient observer of dangerous new times? My impressionistic evidence leads me to affirm the latter.

One day last week the "Nickel Mine Paint Store," a small Amish business housed in a barn along my route, boasted a large plastic banner, alongside the store's more modest hand-painted sign. "Dutch Standard Paints," it announced in bright red italicized letters. This seemed strange, both in spirit and appearance. Such accoutrements of the wider world usually don't achieve this sort of prominent display. Maybe Kraybill and Nolt are right. Perhaps even this venerable *Résistance* is beginning to ebb, as the market marches on.

It is a bright Saturday in January and I meet with a friend from church for lunch. He is a former aide in the Reagan White House, currently at work both locally and nationally on a variety of projects to foster what he calls "civil society." He has lately taken it on the chin in some conservative circles for his critique of the market economy, and I am eager to chat with him about this.

"I am anti-Wal-Mart," he recently confessed in the *Wall Street Journal*, a sentiment not uncommon even in our overwhelmingly Republican county. The developers may be having their way around here much of the time, but the conservative ethos of the area enables many to intuit, however erratically, that these retailers are liquidating virtues and eliminating habits that make our life here what it is.

We discuss this proposition. Can "conservatism" survive when many of its essential qualities and requisite conditions, including individual restraint, deep familial roots, and a sense of place, are under unfaltering assault by corporate capitalism, a system that demands ever more cunning advertising campaigns, bloodless bureaucratized centralization, and community-fracturing uprooting? In America capitalism and conservatism have long been bedmates, of course, but as of late some conservatives have called the union into question; a few have even dared proclaim it illicit. Those outside conservative circles thrill to watch so prominent a pair endure a lover's quarrel. Meanwhile, other conservatives remain on intimate terms with the old, still charming mistress. In the midst of its recent success American conservatism, never an entirely coherent ideology, has become a many-splintered thing.

My friend has a firsthand knowledge of many of these diverging conservatisms, and is particularly troubled by what's become of the "Religious Right." Where many see strength, he finds a void, a failure to understand the cultural landscape, and a resultant inability to advance credible and salutary alternatives. Their political vision, he believes, has little hope of fulfillment, for better or worse.

I share his perspective. Marx famously intuited that under the aegis of capitalism "all that is solid melts into air, all that is holy is profaned," and this seems a hyperbolic but still useful description of not just our nation in the 1990s but contemporary American evangelicalism as well. The Religious Right, envisioning itself as a force to combat our malaise, more often seems a gaudy manifestation of it. Ironically—and this point drives our conversation—self-proclaimed "cultural conservatives" have failed to understand that corporate capitalism, the truly radical and revolutionary force of history, has done more to diminish the possibilities for a rich common life than any of the other "isms" it usually assails—humanism, scientism, feminism, take your pick. In the words of historian Garry Wills, capitalism "is of all things the least worthy of the name conservative," a premise the Religious Right might fruitfully ponder.

My friend's working assumption, though, wards off condescension: this movement's defects are our own; the Religious Right reflects not just an ethereal cultural emptiness—it reflects *us*. Having grown up with consumer capitalism, and in many cases grown it, we evangelicals seem destined to falter in our efforts to serve as a counterpoint to it. Bound both ideologically and economically to the powers that be, we are blind, in good liberal parlance, to conflicts of interest.

We try to imagine ways of effectively addressing these matters, but the hour is late and other obligations call. So we leave the restaurant, and amidst the shiny sea of SUVs and sports cars discover that we have both parked our not-so-shiny vehicles at the back of the parking lot. He wryly notes that he's trying to hide his. It makes me think: perhaps in a culture such as ours we should drive older cars with a sense of honor, see them as symbols of a higher moral order. But I know I was hiding my rusting Toyota as well. As Tocqueville long ago noted, the habits of our American hearts tend to turn community into conformity, a deadly impulse for those who pledge allegiance to another land.

It is the winter retreat of our church's youth group, and during free time on a Saturday afternoon some of the staff strike up a conversation about politics. We sit on sleeping bags in a dingy cabin, the room already ripe with the distinctive scent of junior high boys dorming en masse. The conversation turns to wealth, poverty, and the American church. Our own is a large church, perched along a key artery in an affluent section of the county. It is a meeting place for suburban professionals; numerous lawyers, doctors, professors, and even a few politicians regularly attend.

The very faux clapboard siding seems to secrete Respectability, yet the congregation's deep evangelical impulse cannot be gainsaid. One of the more notable nineteenth-century marriages of politics and religion, the union of Whiggish political economy and evangelical moralizing, is playing out in our midst, a century and a half later. The old Victorian watchwords of domesticity, industry, and charity still spill easily from our lips, and the voluntaristic dynamism of our evangelical forebears resurges in myriad acts of worship and witness.

One staff member recently finished an economics course at the local university. He says, or says that his professor would say, that our church members can justify their extravagant spending with a little macroeconomic casuistry: their expenditures, far from being frivolous, actually fuel the economy, providing labor for those who otherwise might find none and so helping to provide for particular families and individuals. Another staffer, while expressing qualms about the showy nature of these consumptive displays, backs this economic theory, and adds some theological scaffolding to it.

I too want to talk theology, and so throw the old straw epistle of James into the mix. In the second chapter, after warning against showing special privilege toward the rich at the expense of those who have less, James delivers a sharp admonition: "But you have dishonored the poor man." I, gingerly, advance the proposition that while exhibiting faithfulness in manifold ways we, as a church, violate the spirit of this teaching. Although we rent no pews, our ethos seems at odds with the rough egalitarian spirit that Christ intends the church to possess. I put this query to them: Do we, in fact, esteem the poor? Do we do all we can to make "them" feel that "our" church can be theirs? Is theirs?

The discussion heats up, and biography, inevitably, comes to the fore, along with a welter of conjectures and opinions about class, culture, and faith. How do my roots in dirt-farming Appalachia affect my social vision, for better or worse? Do not, in fact, the more educated, cultivated classes have a tutorial role to play for those of lesser fortune? Is it possible, or even desirable, to unite the various classes in a single congregation? The high pitch of our voices, the flashing eyes, the flush of our faces, tell me that this issue is more serious and closer to the heart than our slack treatment of it in formal church settings would suggest.

Perhaps it takes removal from our suburban lair to prompt such discussions. But our brains grow weary as our civility thins, and eventually the kids, back from a rousing afternoon of tubing on manufactured snow, find us again. Our conversation is left on the retreat, the only place in our ecclesial space where this topic seems safe to broach.

For my birthday an old friend from college takes me to a Michael Card concert. Card, long a voice of integrity in the Christian music "industry," as it is known, opens with a few songs, followed by a tongue-in-cheek apology: "Some of you may have come expecting to see lasers and a light show," he remarks, "or at least a hair piece." But this is a no-frills concert: jeans, t-shirts, a bald head, and a lot of music. Glitter and glam didn't draw this crowd. We came for the promise of potent reflection on the meaning of the Word in our time.

More than three hours and many songs later my friend and I seem reluctant to depart from the concert hall, unwilling to leave while we still feel the concert's glow staving off the night. Standing in a foyer we continue our running conversation about Christians in the arts and "contemporary Christian music" (known as "CCM"). Triggered by the emotion of the concert, I find myself verging on passionate as we make our way toward the subject of Rich Mullins, a Christian artist who had died in a car wreck the previous summer. I had just read that according to Reed Arvin, his producer, Mullins kept an extensive journal of musings and confessions that rarely made it into the lyrics of his recorded songs; among these, said Arvin, were things Mullins "couldn't say in the Christian music world." Industry demands, tied as they are to (perceived) consumer taste and sensibility, quarantined more searching reflection and expression.

Learning this struck me deeply, touching all sorts of chords. I had admired Mullins as a pilgrim, an artist who at times ushered listeners to the edge of the profound. His lyrics often carried the scent of the monastery, unusual in CCM, or anywhere. How might his ability to evoke mystery and image the real have been heightened by a more accommodating artistic climate, I found myself wondering, imagining songs and albums left unwritten. Subjected to this editorial surveillance, Mullins could only offer—so long as he chose to work under the auspices of CCM—a guarded glimpse of himself, a publicity shot retouched by executives thinking more like advertisers than honest brokers. That glimpse we caught of the questing sojourner, it turns out, was a bit too polished and slick.

My anger peaks as my friend and I exchange reflections on the consequences of this barren modus operandi. Like me, he as a youth immersed himself in the music of CCM artists like Mullins, hungering for the fruit of honest encounters with God and self. Mullins stood high above many of the others with whom we spent so much time and energy, people to whom we looked for sustenance, inhabitants of an alternative universe that paralleled the world of mainstream popular music. We listened for an echo of our own experience in their art. The older we grew the less we seemed to hear it. At first we heaped blame on ourselves for a spirituality that in this light seemed shabby; gradually we came to sense that the image being delivered by CCM was not (with apologies to Canon) everything. The music and message that once seemed vital and genuine began to sound tinny and hollow. CCM, driven by the measure and ethos of the mass market, had found itself by the mid-1980s comfortably nestled on a procrustean bed, taking a stable of artists and legions of fans along with it.

Our conversation moves naturally from Mullins to Mark Heard, a veteran of the CCM world whose work each of us has developed a deep affinity for. Like Mullins, Heard's life came to an unforecasted end. After a remarkably productive career, in which he recorded fourteen albums in as many years, he died in 1992 of a heart attack, forty years old. Of the many Christian artists who fell under the influence of Francis Schaeffer during the 70s and 80s, he had been the one who perhaps most energetically embodied Schaeffer's call for a theologically rooted social criticism wedded to scrupulous standards of artistic integrity. But by the mid-80s Heard and the magnates of CCM were heading toward divorce. Unwilling to adjust his work to the musical and theological standards of the industry, and frustrated with the pietistic bathos of the broader subculture to which his contractual obligations bound him, he struck out on his own as an artist and producer, forming with the help of a few friends an independent label, Fingerprint Records.

Between 1990 and 1992 Heard recorded three records on his Fingerprint label that unfailingly arrest the imagination, some of the most poignant artistic expression and theological reflection done by any Christian in the last half of the twentieth century. His profoundly American music, folk-rock in the Appalachian vein, was so highly regarded by his peers that following his death Russell compiled a double-CD album of thirty-four artists performing renditions of his songs, largely taken from these last three albums; in 1995 an abridged version of the project, *Strong Hand of Love*, garnered a Grammy nomination. Artists ranging from CCM veterans Randy Stonehill and Phil Keaggy to rockers Michael Been and The Vigilantes of Love to singer-songwriters Pierce Pettis and Bruce Cockburn paid tribute in song to an artist whose ability was enormous, whose vision was profound, and whose honest self-revelation Cockburn, in a moving interview, deemed unparalleled.

Like Mullins, Heard's faith shaped his art, and in a remarkably un-clichéd way. Like Mullins, he felt the squeeze of market demands as he struggled for self-expression and theological integrity. Unlike Mullins, Heard mounted an audible protest against these working conditions and the subculture that sanctioned them; his last records became his testament of another way. On his final album, the white-hot *Satellite Sky*, Heard included "The Big Wheels Roll," a rollicking song in which he told the seemingly autobiographical tale of one man's long struggle to live out his calling in the context of corporate America. At the end of the song the man unleashes his rage:

> He says, "Damn the cool-headed and the setters of goals
> Who can feel no evil, no heat, no cold
> Who wouldn't know passion if it swallowed them whole
> To whom true love is a left-brain risk
> For whom the giving of life is a needless myth
> Who cover their graves with monoliths
> Cool heads prevail, and we'll become extinct
> Mutants too unfit to wish"
> That's the fallout of our fingerprints

By his life's end, Heard had come to believe that the regime of the market moguls represented not just a threat to his own vocation as an artist but also to our very ability to live truly human lives. A harsh critique, to be sure, especially when etched so starkly. But is it accurate? Does it hit at least around on the mark?

Just one rancid cluster of sour grapes, the Christian "realists" might retort, or, more charitably, the unfortunate downside of an economic system that has for the most part served us well. But tonight an opposite conviction gains strength inside of me, fueled by the concert and this conversation. I see embattled prophets denouncing bad-faith compromises with principalities that war against a more Godward vision of the created order. We are ceding ground that is rightfully His, with precious little protest. Nothing countermands these bottom-line dictates—no church, no theology, no god. Some might consider this a useful definition of idolatry.

Now outside the cloakroom, the conversation finally winding down, I feel a touch of guilt for my overly righteous dismissal of the world of CCM, which has indeed—these criticisms aside—served as a conduit for much that is life-sustaining and good, as our experience at this concert attests. But the stories of Mullins and Heard testify of a darker side of the curtain, where a demanding director with overweening authority sits. Theological reflection and honest confession, particularly in the potentially powerful form of art, are being misshaped and falsified.

The market's sieve yields a theology shaped not in the image of God but the "niche" to which it shamelessly panders. In this scheme, instead of imitating God, we mainly succeed in reproducing ourselves. Economics vitiates theology, and we wonder at our poverty. Those so skilled at discerning consumer appetite would do well to heed the aphorism often cited by the evangelical writer Os Guinness: in working out our callings, we are to perform for one audience, the audience of One. The market must not be master.

It is a sunny spring afternoon, perfect for a party. And I end up at one, at a house that sits on the edge of Amish country, in a neighboring county. I strike up a conversation with a newspaper editor who grew up in urban New Jersey. When I tell him where I live his eyes light up: it was his childhood vacation spot! I confess that our county's magnetic appeal to vacationers has long puzzled me. Why not go to the beach? To the mountains? In response, he gestures toward the farmland behind the house. "You don't have this everywhere," he reminds me. For the first time, I think, I begin to understand.

My brother once told me that his landlord, an "English" farmer, was out "hauling Amish." *What?* I asked, picturing a horde of them corralled into a tractor-trailer, Gestapo style. That's what his landlord's wife called it, my brother replied. When he had asked where her husband was, she answered that he was out hauling Amish in his van. The Amish, it seems, sometimes pay the English to take them places their horses cannot. The English who comply seem to imagine this as perhaps a step up from, say, transporting cattle, but probably in the same league. At least their language seems to indicate a valuing of this sort.

The commodification of the Amish is nothing new around here, where larger-than-life statues and etchings of the Amish adorn our highways, luring tourists into every "authentic" Amish (fill in the blank) you can imagine. Here with a few traveler's checks you can watch simulated barn raisings, tour facsimiles of Amish farms, and ride in look-alike buggies through the countryside. One week later you arrive home an expert in Amish lore and culture.

At least this is the way I, cynically, used to see things. But the comments of the New Jersey urbanite prod me to reconsider, to complicate. When free, our choices are usually sourced in the mysteries of attraction. "You don't have this everywhere." And so they come, peering through the commercialized thicket in search of mystery. Perhaps they see in the Amish what I also glimpse: a distinctive way of life, a deeply embedded communal courage, fostered by generations of devotion to a creed, to a few basic ideals, to a manner of being in this world. And perhaps what they see is that for which they also long, but cannot seem to attain.

Opposites attract. "The people walking in darkness have seen a great light." And some of them loved it. Soaked it up. Even discovered themselves made new by it. But the change began with attraction, attraction to something. Something had to be there, something solidly *other*. Something that made their current way of life seem a sham, a hoax, a compromise. Something that promised a luminous possibility they had to try, that whispered of a realm beyond, yet near enough to touch.

Foretaste. Incarnation.

—1998

EARTH

First Landing

Prologue

IT'S MY GRANDMOTHER'S LAMENT, still mournful after all these years, that fills my ears as we pack for the trip. *Your daddy always had a nice garden—till he left for vacation.* Inching past our 400 square feet of (near) produce, I report to my wife a certain queasiness of stomach. I deserve it, I know—or at least my grandmother would think so. Like father like son indeed.

This particular mixed emotion I'm sure my dad knows well. Like his (and my) family several decades past, we are going on vacation, my wife, me, and our three sons, ages nine, five, and not-quite-two. Our destination is one of the places my dad and mom, leaving garden behind, used to take us camping: Virginia Beach, the first place on the North American Atlantic coast where palm trees rise from the earth, a sacred shrine for thousands of Canadians, Americans, and others seeking the restoration sand and sun can give. It is this hope, the hope of restoration, that drives me past our garden.

The soul knows when it has gotten lost. The familiar no longer renews. The normal no longer nourishes. Somehow, we must achieve a different point of relation to that which stands beyond and upon which we are dependent, a point of relation that yields a more satisfying form of connection, mediation, and nurture.

The history of any soul is a tattered one, of course, soiled and ravaged. And, oh: each soul soils and ravages as well. So there is renewal, or there is death.

I seek life. And I seek it on sand.

Virginia Beach, Story I

When I was a kid the name of the place where we camp was simply "Seashore State Park." But at some point that title became a subtitle, now preceded boldly by "First Landing." It's here, the good state of Virginia reminds us, that the founders of the first British colony in North America stepped out to begin, as the momentous sixteenth century was waning, what it is that we've become. This landing, clearly, is to be marked and celebrated.

It is a draw, I admit. Tents dot this cape that extends tenuously into the sea, separating the Atlantic from the Chesapeake, and campers, ankle-deep in the bay, feel the old, old water lapping in. This is the water those venerable pioneers passed through when long ago they landed, so full of hope and disease. For this piece of earth they risked all—a fact that invites meditation.

This year we manage to land while it's still daylight, after a long day of driving from our home in western Pennsylvania. When we had last come, three years before, we pulled in at dusk, only to discover that, yes, we did need reservations. A couple of hours later we set up camp by the headlights' pale glow at TRAV-L PARK instead, surrounded by quiet but spirited Quebecois, several nice pools, a miniature golf course, and live music nightly. It was a fun week. But when we decided to come back this time we opted for the rustic once more and made our reservations. No more fleshpots of TRAV-L PARK for us.

Only one of our sons has memories of this place, and they each feel its mystery as we unpack the van and race the sun stake by stake. Later, driving up the coast in the dark, we come upon a little restaurant under a bridge, order pizza and subs, and head back to the park. After my wife passes out flashlights we stumble through sand, across wooden walkways, and down to the beach. The boys are thrilled. No, they are *way* thrilled. A little sand on the pizza? Tastes fine! Soda spilt on the blanket? Who could possibly care? They shine their lights all around, and discover strangers in the night: little white ghost crabs scurrying furiously across the beach; teenagers trying to be lovers. As we eat our pizza and listen to the water, a thrill passes through us: *This is going to be a great week.* We fall into our sleeping bags wearily but gratefully that first night, and the next morning begin to make our way toward the water.

I have been for most of my life a compulsive reader, from *Danny and the Dinosaur* at the time of my earliest Virginia Beach vacations to *Teaching a Stone to Talk*, a book I've brought along to read in snatches on this trip. But remarkably, at this time, in this moment, my appetite for reading has weakened in dramatic and unprecedented fashion. Even the newspaper I see daily in the camp store holds no attraction. Instead, I lie on the beach, throw my youngest son into the air, race my older ones into the bay, and lie on the beach some more. I look at the sea. I look at the sky. I look at the birds, the crabs, the people. I listen to the wind.

I muse. It's my sense that academics like myself, at least in the humanities and social sciences, have permitted books to furnish the most basic, even final, setting of our lives: not the world as made but the world as *described*. More generally, by our time "culture" in all of its manifestations—whether verbal or material—seems to have become for most Americans that which most fundamentally frames our experience: not (what we call) "nature" but rather the intricate, busy world we humans have constructed with it and upon it.

It is, truly, an astonishing feat, this American world. But I don't think it's an accident, or a mistake, that the verb *repair* still slips off our tongues when we think of something like camping. *He repaired to nature.* Reading *Frankenstein* several years ago, I was struck by the way Shelley has her protagonist, Dr. Frankenstein, seeking refuge and restoration by taking to the outdoors in the midst of his crisis of guilt and despair, heading away from his crazed, sophisticated civilization into a world more wild, primitive, beautiful, and gracious. Our own makings and devisings, even when they don't go awry, are not enough. Renewal comes from somewhere else: this much we know.

At least this is what by this summer I have come to know. For a few days on the cape I'm able to see reading in a radically altered way, as a rich but disembodied form of intelligence, one I've been taught to revere unquestioningly. But what I've never felt so deeply is this one basic fact: *it is not enough.* Nor is this entire "American culture" enough. My soul needs more. My body needs more. *Way* more, and perhaps way less. If the whole project of American civilization at times seems to be to turn the outdoors into the indoors—or to give the outdoors the basic qualities of the indoor life we've devised—then we've rejected eternity for finitude, leaving us in our elaborate houses to suffer our mortality alone.

But family camping is one good way not to be alone. For one thing, the average tent has just one room. One morning I lie on our air mattress and strum my mandolin as our two year old thinks about stirring, warm sun shining through the light fabric. We eventually join the others, make some pancakes, build a fire, and go right from pajamas to bathing suits; the boys sit around shirtless, enjoying the heat. When the sun gets warmer we get into the van and head down to the ocean, riding waves, building castles, eating snacks. Just as we're about to leave the ocean turns suddenly into a fun house; it pounds and pushes and pulls and drives and we stay on, expending with glee all the energy we've got left.

But the cape is not always so hospitable. On an after-dinner walk one evening we see that the sky has turned massively dark and grey to the north of us, over the distant shore of the Chesapeake. "We dodged that one," I announce, relieved. My wife is a bit puzzled by my confidence. "Storms don't travel north to south," I explain. So we sit above the dunes on wooden benches—the best seats in a very big house—and take in a light show of magnificent proportions, well to the north of us. It stretches around the horizon from west to east, and the boys bristle with excitement as lightning turns the black sky white, highlighting the houses and bridges along the bay.

Funny thing: as we get up to leave we notice that the wind has picked up a bit. We proceed a little further, and begin to sense that we're being chased. A minute later we're running like mad down the sandy road, me pushing a toddler in a stroller, trying to get back to the site before It does. We make it and, with the wind beginning to gust, do some quick triage: What goes to the van? What can fit in the tent? What stays outside? And then the big decision: should we take cover in the van or the tent?

Amidst all of this, our two-year-old has managed, Jesus-like, to fall asleep in his stroller, so we decide to place him in his crib and take our chances in the tent. I lie down between our boys and we try to think of things that will make us laugh; eventually, amidst a storm as raucous and harrowing as any I've experienced—it takes it well over an hour to expel its fury—they fall asleep. My wife and I lie awake talking and listening, checking for leaks and feeling a thick wave of humidity paste us to our sleeping bags. As we worry about trees crashing through the tent, we wonder what all the clean and cool folk in the hotels are thinking at this precise moment. *Boring. Bummer!*—words that people living through the likes of this storm could never form.

Later we find out that we had survived what was an unusual (as they say) "weather event": tornadoes had been racing through central Pennsylvania that evening; the storm had indeed been moving from north to south. But when we awoke the next morning we were dry and the sky was sunny. Vacation was still on.

And *wonder* had been redefined. The unwritten word was speaking powerfully. At least for the moment.

Virginia Beach, Story II

Not more than twenty minutes into our long drive to the beach the grating sound of flapping straps against our minivan's windows forces me to pull over along the turnpike. It is my old arch-nemesis, our hard-shell car-top carrier, purchased for an earlier camping trip, coming back at me once more. The display model at Sears had looked so sleek, perfect for our little Nissan Sentra, we thought, so we bought it, and began what turned out to be a tedious, tortured evening of getting the thing ready for the trip. That night proved to be a true omen. Over the years the simple act of locking it has become a source of dread, usually requiring two people five to ten minutes just to get it secured.

We drive hundreds of miles, past multiple roadside crews and through long stretches of cattle chutes. Our kids are (I can hear my mother saying) "wound up." But my wife has taken thoughtful, defensive measures against this quite localized and well-forecasted storm: she begins the slow process of unveiling a series of travel-size toys: Transformers, miniature matchbox cars, action figures. The boys are delighted; they remain reasonably content as we roll along.

Bellies not quite hungry but still in need of lunch, we a couple of hours later pull into a McDonald's in the Baltimore-Washington area. The place is packed, squeezed into a gigantic shopping area on the edge of megalopolis. We're struck by the ethnic and cultural diversity. We're struck by the vehicular diversity. We're struck by the alimentary monotony, and at such a shameless cost, too. We eat and tumble back into the van, hoping for a quick rest-of-the-trip.

We're buoyed along by some good music. For this trip I've purchased Emmylou Harris' *Roses in the Snow*, a remastered CD reissue of her 1980 bluegrass classic. As she sings hopefully of "Green Pastures" we get closer and closer to the shore, moving on to enlarged concrete passageways clogged with traffic, both overground and underground. The kids marvel, a little shakily, as we descend into the bay, protected only by God and engineering ingenuity, and mysteriously close to who knows what ships and sea creatures. We resurface, and mere minutes later arrive at the park.

While the boys excitedly eye the seascape, my wife and I begin a task we take up with deadly focus: what I will come to think of as The Choice. For our 1997 trip here—when the car-top carrier was new—had ended prematurely—abortively even. On the third day a storm blew into the hitherto hot and dry summer, wiped out our tent, and sent us shivering to a hotel. I recall with all the vividness of a nightmare wading through the flash flood to get from the collapsing tent to the car, clasping my oldest son, then two years old, under my rain poncho. Packing up our drenched belongings the next day, I vowed never, *never* to return with a tent that could be so pitifully bested by such weather. So in preparation for our return four years later we purchased the grand-daddy of them all, Coleman's Dakota: a tent so sturdy it makes other tents look like cute playthings. Predictably, it didn't storm on that trip, making the odds pretty good that this time we will get rain.

The Choice, in short, has to be a good one. We have the Dakota. Now we need the right site. After several false starts—space is limited because they're adding more electricity and water throughout the park—we make our decision. It is almost certainly a flood-proof site and, just as important, is only a three-minute walk from the showers and bathrooms. The hauling commences, and by the time we're done we've all but relocated our house: crates of food, bags of clothing, ax and hatchet, lanterns and lights and candles, tarps, stove, charcoal, grill, cooking irons, ice chests, wood, ropes, buckets and shovels, folding chairs, a canopy, sleeping paraphernalia, pots and pans, shoes and sandals and flip-flops, a boogie board, a case of bottled water, and my wife's most prized purchase for this year's trip: the Wonder Wheeler, a four-wheeled contraption for carting almost anything imaginable across the sand.

The real wonder is that the thing actually works: the huge rear wheels make it possible to do more than just drag it across the beach. As always, I'm impressed with my wife's cagey ways, a purchasing agent to make Lewis and Clark take note. From the Hostess Low-Fat Twinkies that my sons and I gobble down to the kid-size eight-ounce cans of Pepsi and Mountain Dew to the bug spray that nightly diminishes our blood loss, our material needs are more than met. The Dakota keeps us dry, and we live it up.

That is, when we are able to overlook the annoying facts of our camping life: I realize, chagrined, that it's actually noisier at our campsite than at our house: a racetrack, known otherwise as Highway 60, runs through the park, and about two hundred yards from our tent. The racers charge along well into the night, obnoxious static for otherwise peaceful campfires and bedtimes. Nor can we easily forget the presence of the United States military at nearby Fort Story, as jets dive and swoop overhead, and granite-like ships move in and around the bay. When at the end of the week we try to do some wash the dryers in the campground laundromat go through quarters like candy before the clothes finally dry. I suffer the ignominy of a reverse farmer's tan (actually a scorching burn); in my haste to supervise the kids in the ocean the first day I forgot to apply suntan lotion to key parts of my torso. And why *do* some campers feel constitutionally required to pump garage rock into the air?

None of these disturbers of the camping peace compares categorically to one my dad suffered on a sunny Sunday thirty years back. As was his custom (and abiding delight), he spent most of the day far out in the ocean. This day he was staying out an unusually long time, well beyond my mother's reach. Finally, as evening neared, a very skinny hippie emerged from the surf and approached my mom with a succinct, stark message: *Your husband is stranded. The tide ripped his trunks off.* My mother loaded up her three children in our big blue Mercury and drove around and around, looking for a shop that would be open on Sunday—it was the early 1970s. She finally came up with a durable navy blue pair, and somehow got them out to her lonely husband. He wore them for years. So far as I know, no ocean ever bested them.

The ultimate annoyance for me this week comes on our last day at First Landing, when I'm once more packing the car-top carrier. As I try, with all the skill I've acquired, to lock it, I feel the key giving way a little too easily. It has broken in two, I discover, and a wave of bitterness overtakes me: it was our only key. After failing to find a locksmith who could cut a new key using the broken pieces, I head to K-Mart and buy heavy-duty bungy cords: I'll strap the thing together, lock or no lock. If not terribly safe from thieves, we're sturdy once more.

"Wilsonburg"

So which is the real story of the week? The desperate quest for spiritual renewal? Or the semi-desperate quest for material survival and, when possible, indulgence? And in our moment and place in history, to what degree are these two vital, deeply human impulses at odds? These are the questions I find myself asking as we leave First Landing and head up the road toward our final destination: Colonial Williamsburg—early American civilization, still in mint condition.

The drive to Williamsburg is a short one—on paper. We cross roads like Powhatan Avenue, named curiously for the Chesapeake chief who in 1607 led a band of some two hundred warriors in a fiery attack on the fledgling Jamestown colony. Awaiting our turn to go down into the bay bridge tunnel, an eerie scene unfolds: an oceanliner is moving directly toward the bridge upon which we are sitting, maybe a quarter-mile away. Although I know it will cross over the section of bridge that is actually underwater, I can't shake the sense that *we're doomed!*, that this mighty sea monster is going to destroy us all, that my family and dozens of others will drown in these waters, finally brought down by the work of our own hands.

But it does of course pass safely over the cars, and an hour later we arrive in Williamsburg. As we lug our belongings into the hotel room, my wife and I are hit with a common sensation: *we're stuck!* Two queen-size beds, some floor space, and not much else. "Camping is way better than this," my wife declares—this after a week of constant motion trying to keep little bodies clothed, clean, fed, and, above all, located. But I agree with her instantly. The hotel seems like a stuffy, if cool, cardboard box after a week on the cape.

To my astonishment, upon entering the room my desire to read returns with a rush—something, anything, a newspaper, book, magazine, *TV Guide, Parade*—as if the very carpet under my feet is singing me back to the printed word. But Williamsburg! This, not reading or cable TV, is our end; our faces are set like flint. In his excited pre-visit state our five-year-old keeps calling it "Wilsonburg." We correct him, and try to prepare him for what he'll be experiencing. And it all begins pretty well, the next morning, after a restless night of air-conditioned sleep. We arrive early at the visitor's center, shell out money for passes, and embark on the journey, which begins with the "Bridge to the Eighteenth Century."

Crossing it, I begin to catch the drift of the official Williamsburg narrative. The bridge, organized as a timeline, is inscribed with messages describing what is happening in America during the era one is (as it were) stepping through. The storylines are not subtle; they veer in two related directions: the growth of modern technology and the enlarging sphere of political liberty. The plaques on the bridge in effect warn the pedestrian that she is indeed going backward in a time, back to a world where women cannot vote and where travel is slow. It is, we're made to see, a world of considerably less freedom than we in our day have come to know.

That about sums up Colonial Williamsburg's spin on the American past. We rush across the centuries and catch Thomas Jefferson giving a speech outside of the governor's palace. He reminds the crowd of "our rights as Englishmen . . . shared throughout the family of man . . . *vox populi, vox dei* . . ." It's all quite rousing; the actor, who is playing Jefferson in a show at the town theater, even takes questions at the end, and gives sharp, clever answers. It's not exactly reality TV, though: the eighteenth-century Jefferson detested giving speeches and whispered them in a voice few could hear. It is actually Patrick Henry–as–Thomas Jefferson we're witnessing. At least they were both Virginians.

But it's clearly not the authenticity of the portrayal that matters here; rather, what matters is the consistency of theme: after leaving Colonial Williamsburg, declares the unwritten mission statement, the visitor will be grounded in those elements of America's colonial past that have delivered us to Today. This grand historical production isn't an attempt to remember the past so much as an effort to remind us of our nation's progressive march. Throughout the day the actors and tour guides rehearse and rehearse the narrative of liberal progress, while also telling, inversely, the story of our technological advance: through their precise, careful reenactments of everyday eighteenth-century life—maneuvering carts pulled by sweaty stench-producing animals, firing the crude artillery, laboring over food preparation, entertaining so simply in the homes—they show us who, thank God, we're not. The main emotion they arouse is pity, both for them and for their forebears: How did these people survive having to do so much *work*? And with so much *clothing* on?

The final walk back across the other side of the bridge confirms my chief response to Williamsburg's America. Moving again toward the twenty-first century, the plaques honor the "Nation-Makers" who have led us to our current prosperity. "Thomas Edison: Turned Night into Day," reads one. "Henry Ford: Gave Americans the Car Keys to Everywhere." Jefferson is pithily described as a "Planter-Free Thinker," who "Made Religion a Matter of Choice." "Democracy" is a "Work in Progress," a marker reminds us: keep movin' on, citizen.

As we leave the town and look for a place to eat, it all seems an embarrassing conceit. Were those eighteenth-century people really so much like us, except for their cumbersome clothing and clinging prejudices? Are we, in turn, so easily their superiors? And, most crucially, does the past so lack mystery? The past *as past* wasn't in the minds of the Williamsburg storytellers, I'm sure—that, after all, is what we fought to be free of.

We end up at a restaurant on the grounds, called "Huzzah!" The boys are exhausted—unmistakably wound *down*. Our nine-year-old slumps to my left, wearing his three-cornered hat with a brilliant scarlet ostrich feather cocked to one side. Our five-year-old clutches a little wooden musket. And our two-year-old sits resting, at last, in the cool air. The wait for our meal is forty-five minutes; it turns out to be glorified cafeteria food—thin gruel after a hard day of traveling back to the eighteenth century.

The Pennsylvanian West

On the long trip home the next morning our garden gradually comes back into focus. *The garden!* Will the beans be engorged, inedible? Did deer, in a feeding frenzy, crash the short wire fence? Have we missed the peas? We'll soon see.

The drive from the ocean to the mountains is beautiful. It's no wonder Jefferson, that Planter-Free Thinker, wove freedom and planting together in his mind, eying up the land across the Mississippi with the wonder of a farmer at harvest time. He insisted, stubbornly, that freedom requires communities of cultivation, a cultivation unifying mind, body, and the earth. The American West will ever serve as his (little understood) monument to another vision of a future America, a land of more active bodies, more simple contentment, more able communities: a true republic. The man, it can safely be said, knew how to dream.

But toward the end of his presidency one of his English contemporaries, taking in the modern, materialist drift, issued a damning pronouncement:

> The world is too much with us; late and soon,
> Getting and spending, we lay waste our powers;
> Little we see in Nature that is ours;
> We have given our hearts away, a sordid boon![1]

It is a matter of degree, Wordsworth sensed: *too much.* "Civilize" we must. We have no choice but to decide upon some way to order our life together on this earth. But the giving of our hearts to *this* form of civilization was surely leading to spiritual disrepair. Both he and Jefferson knew, as we might yet come to know, that our hearts need more, way more, in terms of a satisfying relation to the created order.

I'm looking. I'll get home and pull out my hoe. And I'll read, slowly, the one thing I am bringing home from Virginia: *A Treatise on Gardening*, reprinted by the Printing Office at Colonial Williamsburg and originally published in 1793, written by, simply, "a native of this State." What does one do with an overgrown garden? I don't exactly know. But I suspect he'll have something to say.

—2005

---

1 William Wordsworth, "The World Is Too Much with Us."

Shock and Awe

JAN SWAMMERDAM WAS A young Dutch scientist devoted to God but haunted by bees. Between the years 1669 and 1673 he, with extraordinary intensity, studied the honeybee. He followed it. He sketched it. He probed it. He sliced it. He took notes and made drawings and more, day after day.

The microscope, newly available for such ends, became for him a tool of intimate use, a means to see, marvel, and judge. By 1669, at the age of thirty-two, he had already become a path-breaking figure in entomology with the publication of *Historia Generalis Insectorum*. Narrowing his focus in subsequent years to the honeybee, he was able to establish, finally, that the queen bee indeed has ovaries and is thus responsible for all of the thousands of eggs swarming to life in her hive—just one of many grand mysteries he illumined and enlarged.

Hattie Ellis writes of "the exquisite dexterity of his dissections," as seen in his drawings. His tools were delicately miniature, requiring a microscope for proper sharpening, and his labor was arduous. By the time he brought his bee studies to a close, she notes, his "body and mind were battered; some think he never recovered."

A mere "obsessive"? Or a captive of wonder, perhaps, reaching toward mystery with unyielding, self-sacrificing awe?

It may well be that in the face of the honeybee obsession is the only sane response available, reassuring evidence of true perception. Consider, for instance, this brute fact: that sixteen-ounce honey bear in your pantry exists only because tens of thousands of bees flew some 112,000 miles in a relentless, unquestioned pursuit of nectar gathered from 4.5

million flowers. Every one of those foraging bees was female. By the time the life of each ended—they live all of six weeks during honey-making season—each bee flew about 500 miles in 20 days, the span each lives outside the hive.

As these bees were flying themselves to death, the production inside the hive continued with stupendous efficiency, in the following sequence: bee brings nectar to hive, carried tidily in her "honey stomach." Bee is greeted (cheerfully, one suspects) by a younger, homebody receiver bee, who relieves her of her load. Receiver bee deposits nectar into a cell and proceeds to reduce its water content and raise its sugar level by fanning it with her wings and regurgitating it up to two hundred times, killing microbes along the way. More bees surround this cell and others nearby and fan them with their wings 25,000 times or so, thus turning nectar into honey. When the honey is ripened, wax specialists arrive to cap off the cells. And that is how every single ounce of every single honey pot, bottle, or jar in the world—hundreds of thousands of them—is brought into being.

It invites obsession. "Every gulp of raw honey is a distinct, unique, unadulterated medley of plant flavor; a sweet, condensed garden in your mouth," writes Holley Bishop, an awed amateur beekeeper, trying her level best with ordinary English to capture a miracle.

These bee-and-honey writers are trying to shock us to our senses. As if they can't help themselves, as if seized by a spirit that's compelled them to go forth, they grope for ways to show us what they've been made to see, and what we, the bee fearers and ignorers, have somehow missed. They seek to shock us into encounter, encounter with who we might be and what we on this planet are doing.

Stephen Buchmann, an entomologist writing from the Arizona desert, frames his meditation on the honeybee with a stark passage from Deuteronomy, in which an aged Moses, with a tired and acute sense of desperation, urges the nation of Israel to "choose life," to choose "blessing," so that "both thou and thy seed may live." "Bees and flowers are as vital a part of the intricate web of life as we ourselves are," Buchmann intones. "The question we must ask is: Do we love life enough to save it?"

It is, as ever, a live question. Buchmann harbors dark fears about our ability to answer it well. "Everywhere I've been, the story is the same—the once vast wilderness, from spectacular desert landscapes to lush, steaming rainforests, has been chopped up and reduced to isolated islands." All he knows tells him that this transnational chopping does not bode well for the sustaining of life, whether animal, insect, or plant. "Increasing environmental degradation is diminishing the quality of all our lives as well as our emotional and spiritual well-being," he warns.

Hattie Ellis's graceful and sensitive exploration of the intertwining fates of honeybees and human life begins and ends very much in the same place. A British food writer, Ellis notes that many suspect that pesticides have contaminated the thousands of bee colonies—billions of bees—that have mysteriously died in recent years. The fact that bees are now safer in the city than in the country she takes to be a telling indicator of our morally and ecologically dubious state of affairs. "No bees, no flowers," she reminds. (And for that matter, no bees, less food: scientists estimate that about one-third of our food supply is dependent at some point on the pollinating services of bees. Pesticides, apparently, aren't always clear on who the pests are and who they aren't. A sobering thought.)

Ellis's warning reveals her deepening worry: "If we lose our respect for these miraculous and mysterious insects, it is at our peril. For life is all one: as big as the world, and as small as the honeybee."

Something is happening to us, these writers contend, something big, consequential, alarming. And that something can be traced by following the story of the honeybee. So they each take us, briskly, into the joint journey of humans, honey, and bees through time.

They do so in a way that only underscores how disconnected we've become from our long (and ongoing) history with the natural world. Ellis describes hunter-gatherers who undertook the quest for honey as "a kind of sacramental adventure." She notes that until the seventeenth century the forest's main economic value for Germans lay not just in hunting but also in honey and wax. In ancient Greece the presence of honey was pervasive: "Death, life, mythology, and love: honey slid into them all," she writes.

But no more. Buchmann is nowhere more powerful than when he describes one of his visits to Malaysia, where he accompanies native honey hunters on one of their thieving expeditions. The achievement of the technical feat itself is so laced with ancient stories, myths, and rituals that a Western reader is tempted to think that Buchmann has somehow landed centuries back in time, or perhaps on a different planet. Could this sort of mystical, earthy entwining of the material and spiritual, of taste and transcendence, possibly be happening now, in my lifetime? Yes. But in a land far, far away.

No wonder that when Ellis describes the "rising rationality of the eighteenth and nineteenth centuries," one senses that, for her, something ominous is happening. Fading were the days when a bee sting might be received as direct—*very* direct—communication from a family member suffering in purgatory, as was commonly believed in France. Rising were the days when the lives of countless rural people were "shaken out of rhythm by the 'march of progress.'" Modern capitalism, empowered by modern science, would separate bees from people in a world ever more flat, mechanical, and, in her word, "homogenized." And bees would come to represent "an old-fashioned idyll as factories churned and cities spread," she writes.

Tammy Horn's ambitious book *Bees in America: How the Honey Bee Shaped a Nation* takes the reader deep into the American side of this sprawling story. Bees had once been so present in the public imagination, she shows, that English gentry made elaborate, effective use of bee-inspired analogies to shape the colonizing of America. "Hiving off" to start a new colony was a demonstrably natural endeavor for a prosperous and efficient bee-like people, they argued. Milk and honey were sure to flow in the New World, provided they followed the bees' industrious example (and provided they transported cattle and bees to the New World, which they did). Horn reads a certain malignity of intent in their use of, as she puts it, "a biological model to justify a social phenomenon."

Nowhere is this seen more clearly than when these aristocrats referred to the poor as "drones," the male bees whose sole productive function is to mate with the queen, after which they die a quick (but one hopes glorious) death. Those drones who suffer through the summer without a royal tryst are summarily put out of the hive by the more industrious females come cold weather, these Englishmen underscored: a word in season to the criminally unproductive. "Many American social policies—so conscious of work, labor, and time—are still based on the beehive model first adopted during the seventeenth century in

England," Horn contends. "Unfair land acquisition, poor treatment, disenfranchisement": these were, in colonial America, "the real consequences of the beehive rhetoric."

Eventually Enlightenment came, though for Horn, like Ellis, its major effects on the honeybee, honey itself, and beekeepers, were woeful. Her sympathies clearly lie with the author of a remarkable 1874 letter to the *Pittsburgh Leader*, who lamented the passing of a day when "a 'bee course' was legal tender, almost." But now "Everything's changed. . . . Everybody wants to speculate and monopolize things nowadays. . . . You can't even take a hound or two for a little harmless sport any more without being hauled up for trespass, for somehow or another somebody's bound to inform on you. But of course, bee hunting suffers like everything else that was originally intended for man's benefit." Horn notes, simply, that as the twentieth century neared there were "ever-increasing conflicts between civilization and nature," as the "agrarian lifestyle" so basic to the nation's (and, for that matter, all nations') past "clashed with the ever-encroaching industrial one."

Of these writers, Bishop is the writer least bothered by this now-completed encroachment, and the one who gives us the best glimpse of the fate of beekeeping in it. Her *Robbing the Bees* is structured around a year in the life of a commercial beekeeper, a Floridian named Donald Smiley, who makes a middling wage collecting, with obsessive delight, exquisite kinds of honey from his millions of bees. But Bishop's breezy style seems at odds, in fact, with the sort of world she's describing, for Smiley faces enormous challenges trying to keep his treasured enterprise afloat. "Each minute he doesn't have all of his supers [i.e., the wooden boxes that contain the honeycombs] deployed to catch the strongest flow, he's losing money. Commercial beekeeping is a game of musical chairs with Mother Nature at the turntable."

Indeed, serious biological problems, stemming from mites—the varroa mite, to cite one example, killed 90 percent of Florida's bees in one year—and beetles have been multiplying. And it's not just Mother Nature who's doing the damage: besides battling the contagion of herbicides and pesticides, commercial beekeepers have been fighting to keep the flow of cheap foreign honey from putting them under. Perhaps the encroachment isn't complete after all.

In the face of this profoundly altered world, Ellis's hope, which elegantly shapes her book, lies in a revival of more robust forms of local life. "The rediscovery of local foods is not about pretending to live in a long-gone past, a time when people were more limited to the food produced in their area," she corrects. Rather, "eating local honey makes your backyard richer."

Such poignant longing for a richer way of life animates each of these writers. In the case of Buchmann, it takes on an unabashed spiritual dimension, as he speaks ardently of "our deep, sustaining, almost sacramental relationship with the natural world"—what he, following E. O. Wilson, terms *biophilia*. He turns to the bee as a means of awakening. In order to set our way straight once more, he implores, we need "the recovery of that sense of wonder and amazement we all experienced as children when first discovering the plants and animals that surround us. I hope," he confesses, "that an intimate look at the enduring bond between bees and mankind . . . will rekindle that sense of wonder."

One cannot help but suspect, though, that the sort of metaphysical minimalism that frames these hopes is too small a frame to support so large a burden. How far, in the end, can secular awe take us toward the spiritual and moral renewal to which these authors call us?

For, as much as they disdain the effects of modernity on our relationship to the natural world, these writers—Buchmann, Ellis, and Bishop in particular—are carried into the past by a distinctly modern, pragmatist wind. Blown back in search of practices that offer a genuinely alternative way of experiencing material reality, they all the while remain curiously uninterested in engaging the big ideas of those times. Can the practices and rituals they find so appealing be widely sustained apart from our accepting, in some fashion, those ideas, and the One who stands behind them?

Jan Swammerdam would not think so. He, the obsessed seventeenth-century Dutch bee lover, had, it turns out, another love, and another faith. Poised at the edge of modernity, living during a time when Enlightenment still held the divine and the material in magnetic tension, Swammerdam could not allow himself to rest easily in his fascination with insects. "Sir," he once wrote to a friend, "I present you the omnipotent finger of God in the anatomy of the louse." The insects he studied compelled him to look above, and beneath. Struggling anxiously to reconcile his loves, for a time he forsook his scientific studies to join a religious community. But in the end he came back to the honeybee. His posthumously published and most celebrated book, *Bible of Nature*, captured powerfully, Ellis writes, his "devotion to God and his creations."

The way to devotion to God always leads through that which is made. There is no other way. "I have noticed in my life," the Sioux writer Brave Buffalo observes, "that all men have a liking for some special animal, tree, plant, or spot of earth. If men would pay more attention to these preferences and seek what is best to do in order to make themselves worthy . . . they might have dreams which would purify their lives."

Who can doubt that the world needs such purification? Who can fault those who dream of it? We, who feel so much more at home in big-box stores than in the company of bees, may yet see awe and wonder opening the way to our deliverance. And on our way, we may just find ourselves following the mysterious buzzing bees, eyes brightened by the gold to which they lead.

—2006

Food™

REMARKABLY, HERE IN THE twenty-first century we still find ourselves directing our ever accumulating know-how toward the pesky matter of food. It's the problem that won't go away.

Boston Globe columnist Ellen Goodman, a reliable barometer of matters political and cultural, registers the mood. In an age when "storybook children who used to visit grandparents on their farms now visit them at golf course condos," she writes, "freedom from the farm is starting to feel like disconnection. . . . We've gone from raising crops to worrying about them."

It's a worry that seems altogether rational. "Industrial fishing practices have decimated every one of the world's biggest and most economically important species of fish," reports the *Washington Post*'s Rick Weiss. The Scripps Howard News Service warns that due to the heavy use of pesticides consumers should "Thoroughly wash produce," and "Peel fruits and vegetables like cucumbers and apples whenever possible." In 2004 The National Academy of Sciences issued a report warning about the dangers of genetically modified organisms and calling for more effective "bioconfinement strategies." A study issued in February by the Union of Concerned Scientists found that crops of maize, soybeans, and canola have been "pervasively contaminated with DNA sequences from GM [genetically modified] varieties." A U.S. Department of Agriculture study discovered that "60 percent of the 35 major beef slaughtering and processing plants fail to meet federal standards for preventing E. coli," leading annually to an estimated 76 million illnesses, 325,000 hospitalizations, and 5,000 deaths.

And this, recall, is in the United States. Extend your vision beyond our southern shores and the food circumstance worsens dramatically, as a visit to Haiti, Mexico City, or the Sudan will attest. To be sure, in terms of food production the twentieth century figures as the most remarkable in history, when the triune juggernaut of science, government, and commerce carried agronomic expertise and abundant grain to hungry people everywhere. Experts judge that world famine was averted due to these efforts, and if so we should marvel, humbly, at this feat. But the economic and technological trajectory of that century continues, and where it is taking us is by no means certain. Many seeming agricultural gains are now netting losses, or at best breaking even, and the emerging record of twentieth-century agribusiness is revealing error, flaw, and corruption in all arenas—scientific, economic, political. Nonetheless, the juggernaut rolls on. To where? That's where the controversy begins.

Mark L. Winston wants to put us at ease. A biologist at Simon Fraser University in British Columbia, he takes on issue after issue in a moderating, judicious key in *Travels in the Genetically Modified Zone*. Along the way his frequent references to "communal comfort zones" and "potential middle grounds" tip us off both to the explosive nature of the terrain and to his own interest in defusing it.

The former U.S. trade representative Robert B. Zoellick's rhetorical blast at the European Union exemplifies the sort of thing Winston is up against. "European antiscientific policies," Zoellick thundered in January 2003, "are spreading to other corners of the world." Zoellick, it turns out, was referring to the EU's longstanding ban on genetically modified food, which, the Bush administration claimed, is influencing impoverished African nations to reject the importation of American crops, despite the threat of starvation.

Is genetically modified (GM) food—or, as the Brits have dubbed it, "Frankenfood"—the serious threat so many Europeans believe it to be? Winston thinks not; if anything, transgenic technology for him is part of the solution to a problem far more ominous: the reliance of industrial agriculture on the heavy use of pesticides, which, unlike GM foods, are already known to be hazardous to humans. Ever since scientists in the 1980s succeeded in inserting virus-and vermin-destroying genes into the DNA of corn, soybean, and other staples, the hope of pesticide-free corporate agriculture has become a possibility, and North American farmers have been voting with their plows ever since: between 1996 and 2001 alone the number of GM crops in the U.S. increased from four million acres to 125 million acres, 68 percent of the worldwide total of GM crops.

Critics of this shift have not been silent, and to his credit Winston treats them with more than a veneer of respect. He acknowledges that "science as a discipline has not responded well to moral objections," including the notion that "genetic engineering is the sole province of the deity." In the end, though, his political and epistemic home is the university laboratory; he is convinced that what that perch enables him to see is sufficient to make moral and political judgments on these matters. When he announces that "Today we are selectively, deliberately, and surgically, reinventing the plant world," and when he revels in the emergence of "an even more complex, multinational, and corporate way of doing farming," we get the picture: by his lights, it's an upward course we're on. Problems remain for experts to solve, but for the most part we have reason to remain hopeful. The biggest problem of all, by Winston's lights, may simply be persuading the masses to respect Science and the world it has made.

Richard Manning's vision of the cultural and political landscape differs markedly, even if his conclusions on genetic engineering line up in some ways with Winston's. A journalist whose work centers on environmental concerns, Manning's *Food's Frontier* is an account of the McKnight Foundation's recent efforts to bolster agricultural efforts through its funding of nine projects around the world. The foundation teamed up scientists from nations as diverse as China and Chile with scientists based in American universities in order to work on regional problems that, if solved, would substantially improve the food circumstance of each particular place.

With quiet sympathy Manning etches the dance between culture and agriculture that is our fate as a species, showing through story after story that to disrespect the latter is to endanger the former. The "Green Revolution," the mid-twentieth-century agricultural boom that staunched famine throughout the world through industrial farming, has run out of gas, he contends: it's productivity has been leveling off as its methods are proving to be, in the telling euphemism, "nonsustainable." Meanwhile, the world's population continues to soar; some predict that the demand for food will double by the year 2020.

Needless to say, the pressure is on to provide solutions, and organizations like the McKnight Foundation are responding. Manning for the most part likes what he sees. The "second green revolution," he hopes, will center on genetic modification made possible through the collaboration of researchers and farmers in discrete locales, rather than in distant laboratories. "The Green Revolution at its most fundamental level treated all the world the same," he writes, "but the lessons being learned in agriculture now are all local." His own writing delightfully reflects that conviction, as when he travels up to Mexico's Sierra Norte de Puebla and finds local markets so rich and meals so tasty that he ends up reexamining his understanding of poverty. He discovers, in this region deemed unuseful by the broader national and global market, people who cultivate 250 species of edible plants and 300 more that have medicinal uses. What, in the end, makes one wealthy?

So Manning embraces the local, and especially the rural, but not due to a romantic fantasia of pastoral bliss. Rather, it's the sight of Mexico City's millions living in squalor that turns him away from the city for hope. Instead of going the route of "development," he urges those devoted to ameliorating the crisis of global poverty to embrace a rural, decentralizing vision, in which networks of organizations serve needy people around the world through practices that aid particular peoples and their habitats. While skeptical of the wonder-working power of genetic engineering, he recognizes that, as he puts it, the "genie is already out of the bottle, way out"; best now to seek to harness it with exceeding care, always making the health of the local the measure of the technology's worth.

For now, Manning's vision of a global network of voluntary nongovernmental organizations helping to nurture local agriculture is but a hope. The world we live in, whether it be western India or western Pennsylvania, is dominated by multinational corporations with huge stakes in the global food industry—and huge stakes in preserving their place in it. They are committed to going wherever humans need food. Which is of course everywhere.

The tenacity with which these corporations have pursued the grand prize of controlling the global food supply is revealed with revolting clarity in two recent books, *Lords of the Harvest: Biotech, Big Money, and the Future of Food*, by Daniel Charles, and Marion Nestle's *Food Politics: How the Food Industry Influences Nutrition and Health*. Upon reading them, the question that comes to mind over and over is, why are we trusting these people with our *food*, of all things?

Nestle, a New York University nutritionist, flatly states that "nutrition becomes a factor in corporate thinking only when it can help sell food." Years of working in the academic, corporate, and political spheres has given her the evidence she needs to proclaim "a national scandal," featuring food companies that "routinely place the needs of stockholders over considerations of public health," not at all unlike the (only recently) disgraced tobacco companies.

Since the leading causes of death in the United States now find their common source in what she describes as "chronic diseases associated with excessive (or unbalanced) intake of food and nutrition," one would hope that federal and state governments would step up to provide leadership, a clarifying voice for its confused citizens. But Nestle tells a different story in alarming detail: of federal officials and government agencies succumbing to corporate influence, and of corporations that make it their explicit aim to co-opt nutrition experts into supporting the products the market (allegedly) demands.

The examples she provides astound. She quotes from a corporate manual that instructs its reader that the experts brought in to monitor the company's work "must not recognize that they have lost their objectivity and freedom of action." She notes that the UC Berkeley Department of Plant and Microbial Biology in 1998 sought and obtained an exclusive partnership with an industry partner, Novartis, in order to secure steady and deep funding; the agreement gave Novartis the right to not only select participating faculty but also to review the faculty's research results prior to publication. The question Nestle leaves us with merits insistent consideration: if neither the government nor the academy nor the corporate world is giving itself over to fostering public health, who is?

Daniel Charles corroborates Nestle's tale. At the heart of his story, told superbly in *Lords of the Harvest*, lies Monsanto, a massive, utterly domineering multinational chemical and biotech company. The fact that even as it aspired in the 1980s to create "a bright, clean, hopeful new world" insiders knew it as a "tumultuous place that chewed up talent and tossed it aside" might warn us not to look to it for civic hope. "They promised to transform a world they barely understood," Charles writes damningly.

Monsanto was among the pioneering companies that created and marketed the first genetically modified plants. Along the way it fought hard and dirty against any observers, activists, and critics who voiced seemingly sane concerns about, in Charles' troubling term, "the growing corporate domination of plant life." One former Monsanto CEO went so far as to admit that while the company was developing the GM crops with which it was intending to change the world, "There wasn't even one discussion of the social implications. I never thought of it." The only harm Monsanto was consistently concerned about was the harm done to its bottom line. This is how we change the world?

Both Nestle and Charles deliver devastating perspectives on the recklessness with which the exorbitantly financed, do-or-die world of global capitalism has approached the most basic task of provisioning. Both authors rightly despise key aspects of that world while resigning themselves to working within its limits. But is there another path? Is making the world safe for industrial capitalism all that's left? Or might Christian faith call for a more excellent way?

The mammoth organizations to which we've outsourced our provisioning "love control, efficiency, and predictability," Charles observes—loves that may well be the source of their (and our) eventual demise. But Charles goes on to draw a contrast more illuminating than he perhaps knows: agriculture, he notes, "is a holdover from an earlier era; it's dirty, messy, and unpredictable."

Agriculture, that is, is of a piece with other beloved, utterly irreplaceable forms of local life: families, neighborhoods, towns, marriages. In each of these, to avoid the mess is to avoid the thing itself—tempting, for certain, but surely not satisfying of our truest ends, and so not truly satisfying to *us*.

A simple question: might it be that when a people seeks to evade the everyday, utterly elemental practices of agriculture they end up evading life itself? Put differently, might it be that what theologians call the "cultural mandate" of Genesis 1–2 is doomed to fail apart from the foundation of a faithful, collective enacting of the *agricultural* mandate the Lord first gave Adam: to tend and care for the earth in discrete, local places?

The Indian physicist and environmental activist Vandana Shiva, despite her religious differences, would affirm the moral necessity of a carefully calibrated symbiosis between culture and agriculture, region by region, place by place. In her book *Water Wars*, she looks at her own country and suggests that "The nonsustainable, nonrenewable, and polluting plastic culture is at war with civilizations based on soil and mud and the cultures of renewal and rejuvenation." She sees the interplay between culture and agriculture as fundamentally a religious issue, as does the writer Barbara Kingsolver, whose pursuit of this same renewal and rejuvenation has led her family to try to grow much of its own food. In an arresting confession, she explains, "I'm not up for a guilt trip, just an adventure in bearable lightness. I approach our efforts at simplicity as a novice approaches her order, aspiring to a lifetime of deepening understanding, discipline, serenity, and joy."

It's a confession we all might consider making—a deeply human confession, one that promises to take us into unpredictable places, where gardens grow and neighbors dwell. Perhaps even places where a Maker walks with his creatures, and where the hungry find food. Good food.

—2003

POLITICS

Realism against Reality

IN A 1967 BOOK review fraught with Cold War anger and anxieties, the historian and social critic Christopher Lasch denounced a political stance he dubbed "vulgar realism," a way of seeing that, by his lights, had locked up the American political imagination and paralyzed the body politic. By smugly resisting any thrusts for structural change in American political life, self-proclaimed "realists" were pronouncing a covering blessing on all the nation had by the 1960s become. This so-called realism, Lasch warned, actually amounted to "the abdication of moral judgment, the appeal to some abstract and impersonal necessity which is supposed to make questions of right and wrong irrelevant." "What we need," he concluded, "are books critical of political messianism but equally critical of 'consensus.'"

Four decades later, that need persists—but especially the criticism of consensus. The American "consensus" and the "realism" that underpins it have changed shape in the post–Cold War world, to be sure, but the broad political and ideological trajectory that so troubled Lasch rumbles on, taking us relentlessly toward its end.

The hope, of course, is that our system will lead us to an end in the Aristotelian sense, with progress, prosperity, and happiness rewarding those who give themselves over to our way of pursuing life. But the forms of progress, prosperity, and happiness our civilization has in the past century delivered suggest, sadly, that it's another end that we've been moving toward.

Estimates of our mortal sins differ. Some point to the unprecedented forms of human bondage developed by the West as most profoundly reflective of the condition of our collective soul, while others are more unsettled by the peace we've made with destroying human beings in the womb as (remarkably) a way of life. Christians of varying sorts have affirmed both judgments, while citing other civilizational pathologies: deepening and bewildering forms of sexual promiscuity, a mass idolatry of technology, the erosion of neighborhoods and other forms of local community, and the degradation of the earth itself. On the American watch, the "home" has morphed into a self-contained entertainment center, aging has become a source of shame, and humans have been reduced to "individuals," creatures who don't mature so much as simply exist, doing what they will.

The Christian realist sighs. "There you go again, refusing to affirm the good we've achieved. And you expect too much from a race that is, after all, corrupt. The evil of our day isn't such a departure. And the good you won't let yourself see is worth more than you grant. Behold the wheat; behold the tares. Besides, would you *really* choose to live at any other time?"

Knockout blow delivered. Head back in book. Peace restored.

Except for that alarm that must be sounding somewhere, vibrating down a darkened hall toward the realist's sleepy soundproof den. It's the alarm that goes off whenever we mistake the counterfeit for the real, whenever we grant substance to shadows, whenever we laud the compromise as the ideal. As the deception worms its way in, despair, with a quiet air of righteousness, begins to justify its presence. How? With an arsenal of "realistic" arguments.

What is wrong with this "realism"? It is, most fundamentally, an offense against reality itself: the reality of our true creaturely ends. In its Christian guise, it denies not that we are made to live in distinct, particular ways, but rather the belief that we can, and should, seek to inhabit them. Its way of honoring the ideal—by burying it far in our past or placing it far into our future—actually removes the ideal from our grasp. If the true task of any civilization is to guide its corporate life toward the ways in which we as a race were meant to live, this realism blinds us to those ends by constantly reminding us of what we are not; the effect is to make us aim lower and lower and lower, until transcendence of our current circumstance becomes a mere act of fantasy—if it remains an activity at all.

In its secular guise, "realism" takes on an even more perverse quality: it erases the hope of any end that is fundamentally different from whatever vision of life currently lies in our sights. What is, is—a condition some may celebrate and some may deplore; either way, an enlarged sphere for diabolical mischief emerges, as in the absence of transcendent purpose the very meaning of human existence becomes the plaything of the great mind-shapers of the age. "The abdication of Belief / Makes the Behavior small," observed Emily Dickinson—small, and so easily manipulated by anyone with an ounce of power.

Of course, we aren't consciously extending invitations to the demonic when we succumb to "realism." We, weary of pressing toward Belief, settle into a state that seems simply more sane, and less exhausting. Or we conclude that we're maturing, and ease into our new digs with something like gratitude but more like relief, taking comfort in the "ambiguities" and "complexities" of life in these times. Possibly we just follow the traces of those elders who have instructed us in the ways of the world, and as a matter of habit peer suspiciously at those who doubt the wisdom of that which has brought us to this point. Whatever the pathway to it, calling this stopping place "home" signals the deadening of fundamentally healthy and necessary human impulses: the longing to be that which we are not but could (and should) become.

In this particular moment, we (middle-class) Americans boast, without usually thinking about it, a triumphal form of realism, as what we're sure will become the American millennium glides onward, despite occasional setbacks. We glory in our power, we delight in our pleasures, we marvel at our conveniences. Cheering the flag, we pity those who lack our attainments, and hide our doubts somewhere in the rushing caravan of career, school, and the dozens of other assorted activities we call our life. But every now and then one question (asked in many forms) manages to sound loudly enough to slow us down: *is this really life?* If "civilization" is meant to help us to choose life, why does it smell so much like death around here?

The simple posing of these questions makes one thing clear: maintaining a civilization is far easier than pursuing our truest ends. Any civilization tends as a matter of course to turn its members toward an elemental dependency of body and soul on the grand, overarching political and economic system it has developed to sustain and organize human life. This dependency is, crucially, fundamentally religious: an offering of the self to that which it believes will deliver what it needs. Civilization, rather than being a means to an end, becomes an end in its own right, and so a god. In the name of this cult(ure), we end up justifying massive moral, political, and intellectual compromise for the sake of the lower-order pursuits—pleasure, painlessness, power, tranquility, identity, or simply survival—that civilization affords.

Take the omnipresent corporations that, with their thundering promise of provision, rule over our civilization, and, increasingly, our world. Despite their vaunted version of prosperity, the mavens of corporate capitalism have done little in the past two centuries to inspire confidence in their ability to understand what the earth and its people truly require, much less evidence that the corporations will someday operate in a decent fashion, honoring our Maker and prospering our progeny. Rather than embracing nurture and thrift, global capitalists, with legions of the best and the brightest in their employ, have operated at best solipsistically and at worst rapaciously, willing to exploit all that we hold dear—from children to mountains to language to health itself—for their self-absorbed ends. This is the pathway to life? This is provision?

We know it's not. But this knowledge we, understandably, would rather repress. So here we are, one hundred and some years into a life scheme whose promises are as hollow as the TV networks that deliver them. Our civilization—our religion—is failing us. Badly.

What to do?

"It is no principle with sensible men, of whatever cast of opinion, to do always what is abstractedly best," advised John Henry Newman as he was attempting to launch a Catholic university in Dublin in the 1850s. "Where no direct duty forbids, we may be obliged to do, as being best under circumstances, what we murmur and rise against, while we do it. We see that to attempt more is to effect less; that we must accept so much, or gain nothing; and so perforce we reconcile ourselves to what we would have far otherwise, if we could."

What may seem at first glance to be just one wordy Victorian's restatement of the realist's credo—*Be satisfied with compromise*—on second glance looks less "realistic" and more useful. Note especially that hopeful phrase "what we murmur and rise against." Even as Newman chafes against the limits he knows will force him to accept less than he desires, his longing for the good, for the ideal, pulses strongly within. Even as he warns implicitly against what Lasch in 1967 termed "political messianism," he guards against giving the "consensus" undue honor and so capitulating to that which will weaken his own commitment to see vitality and grace embodied in everyday life. Compromise, on this vision, is driven solely by a hope for real (if incremental) progress toward the ideal. Communal health, Newman knew, is measured not simply by the achievement of the ideal, but, even more crucially, by the image of the ideal the community erects.

So what kind of civilization constructing should we give ourselves to? Which compromises will nurture life, and which will endanger it?

Such decisions, if they are to be morally sound and politically effective, require the consent of the communities affected and involved. Only those who have achieved intimacy with a given community can discern well the nature of the threats to it and envision its most hopeful prospects for change. Towns, churches, schools, businesses, counties, neighborhoods, colleges, families: each must be led by elders (the precise opposite of "consultants") with a wisdom both broad and deep, men and women guided by an abiding affection for the health of the particular place and its people—and by an adequate understanding of health itself.

The critical question for all of us who in this moment of our civilization's history seek such health must be: *how can we extricate ourselves from degrading dependencies and attachments and replace them with more human, life-giving forms of support and connection?* This question forces us to see that our dependencies and attachments both reflect and dictate our true religion—that upon which we most fundamentally as creatures rely. Given the religious quality of our dependencies, it follows that any shifts in them will ramify in an array of cultural directions: into the realms of art, ideas, education, economics, agriculture, manufacturing, research, and more. Understanding the nature of our cultural crisis as at heart religious prepares us to see, too, that the work of extrication and incarnation will be intensive, demanding far more than "rational" decision making and good "strategy." The roots of our contemporary assumptions about reality run deep, and uprooting them will require a form of earthy spirituality inimical to the gnostic materialism of our day.

Such spirituality finds its ground in the abiding reality of goodness, a goodness sourced in a Creator who is present, and who sacramentally draws those who drink of his goodness into a manner of living that more faithfully and wonder-fully reflects our creaturely estate. Because goodness presides and prevails, we gain the courage to pursue another way, defying the common sense of the day with acts that testify of another wisdom, a different vision, a deeper justice: acts as simple as planting a garden, writing a poem, or walking to a church; acts as grand as running for office, starting a grocery store, or having another child. In living our faith in such ways, we place always before us the reminder that the miracle that deserves our deepest respect and allegiance is not what we as a civilization have done with the gift of life, but rather the enormous, mysterious fact of life itself.

A certain variety of realist will scoff at the political drift of this vision, even while agreeing with the contours of the cultural critique. As they tell the story of our civilization, these realists tend to give history ontic status: their overwhelmingly bitter and bleak narrative of our decline and corruption makes any turn-around seem impossible; potential political thrusts, however fledgling and tentative, are straitjacketed into paralysis—our woeful story is, after all, the sum of who we have become, and no movement forward is conceivable. "Turn Left at the Renaissance," runs the headline of one self-consciously "conservative" magazine, implying a demise so ancient and deep that misery and despair can only follow.

This view is a fallacy. The past does not exist. What exists is the present, shaped profoundly by the past but made possible, moment by moment, by a goodness sourced in a Maker who bids us to reflect his glory, to embody his righteousness, to love his justice, *now*. *This* reality must be the starting point for our politics. Sometimes it may require us to do the culturally unconservative thing of bringing not peace, but a sword. Always it will require a gritty faithfulness to the beauty and justice of a God whose presence alone ensures our hope.

It is true: most overarching historical narratives of our life on this plane will be bleak—or should be. But the same narratives should also feature stories of those whose love of goodness and justice drove them to embody another way. Occasionally, they triumph.

When they do, something called *shalom* happens: a peace social and personal at once takes root, fostering the possibility of freedom for those within their reach. They become a foretaste of a fuller shalom yet to come, a promise of a way of life pure, rich, and satisfying. Until that day, they live as Dwight Macdonald once quipped of the radical: "pleased if history is also going his way" but "stubborn about following his own road." The road, in this case, is the pathway to our final reality: true realism. It's the journey that begins when someone dares to believe Christ knew what he was doing when he issued that troubling yet hopeful command: *Be ye perfect.*

—2004

The Birkenstock Brigade

A STRANGE THING HAPPENED to Rod Dreher in the summer of 2002. From the bowels of the modern conservative movement, he, a young writer for the *National Review*, published an online column that rang out as a call to arms. In "Birkenstocked Burkeans: Confessions of a Granola Conservative" Dreher disclosed that he and his wife "have more in common with left-wing counterculturalists than with many garden-variety conservatives." Among the telltale signs were a taste for organic food, a deep suspicion of big business, and a conviction that environmental conservation is a great good. "Somebody's got to pioneer these things" on the right, he declared. "Dare to dream, you Birkenstocked Burkeans, and pass the hippie carrots."

They did more than dream—they deluged him with email. The article sped through cyberspace and into the homes of thousands of like-minded folk, leading Dreher, less than four years later, to enlarge his modest column into a pop manifesto with a book-length subtitle: *Crunchy Cons: How Birkenstocked Burkeans, Gun-Loving Organic Gardeners, Evangelical Free-Range Farmers, Hip Homeschooling Mamas, Right-Wing Nature Lovers, and Their Diverse Tribe of Countercultural Conservatives Plan to Save America (or at Least the Republican Party).*

The subtitle is more than cute—it's instructive. As its mock grandiosity hints, it's not the usual political movement for which and to which Dreher is trying to speak. Rather than outlining a policy-driven program, he's more concerned, he states, to explore "a sensibility, an attitude, a fundamental stance toward reality," one that might lead more and more toward a "secession of sorts from the mainstream" in order to "conserve those things that give our lives real weight and meaning."

At the very center of this seemingly countercultural vision is an effort to, in his words, "see life sacramentally," to understand "the physical aspects of our lives"—food, place, woods, lakes—"as being inseparable from spiritual reality" and, indeed, the mediator of it. Sacramentality thus emerges as one of Dreher's two key thrusts, whether he is criticizing contemporary culinary practice (beware the "better-living-through-chemistry propaganda") or coming out on global warming ("the most serious crisis overtaking mankind as a result of our refusal to live within our means"). With intelligent enthusiasm Dreher urges a reorientation at the deepest levels of perception.

His other major thrust is less convincing. Think of it as "the hunt for true conservatism." Throughout the book Dreher persistently calls the reader toward a life that more faithfully hews to the conservative tradition in which he, hippie carrots notwithstanding, continues ardently to position himself. While conservatism, he believes, is ultimately about "creating anew," the economic practices and cultural habits of Republicans consistently militate against a renewal of a more moral, sensible way of life. So Dreher bombs away at the GOP mainstream. The "big-haired Republican types," the "Babbitts," the contented members of the "Party of Greed": these receive just as much (if not more) of his rhetorical fire as the liberals do; indeed, he sees the two sides as in most respects the same, united in a reckless, shallow, heedless individualism.

Dreher's intent to erect a truer standard is refreshing. And it's refreshing because it's right. A profoundly sacramental vision must indeed lead us to straighten all aspects of our lives. Apart from a deeply rooted sacramental consciousness humans live with a disposition not to receive grace but to dispose of its effects. Cultures that neglect to cultivate a sacramental experience of the world default necessarily to an instrumentalist consciousness, with its narcissistic, self-deifying impulse toward consumption, whatever the cost.

But in the face of our persistent failures as a race to achieve this sublime vision of earthy, heavenly peace, how are we to live? This is where Dreher's political tradition fails him. For in this broken world, *sacrament* must always be complemented by that other deeply christological, eminently political S-word: *sacrifice*, the laying down of one's life in behalf of the other. Crucially, outside of his vision for the family, Dreher's political landscape is devoid of any such thing. If this is all the further his conservatism takes us, it's not far enough.

Take a typical passage: Dreher warmly remembers a house that made him "feel at home in the world and enchanted by goodness and harmony," and urges us to think about homemaking, architecture, and aesthetics in this light. Given the sorry mixture of glitz and dullness that today defines our look and style, it's a word in season, to be sure. But are there not other dimensions of our common life that citizenship— whether Christian or American—requires us to consider, especially in our age? In a book about fundamental moral and spiritual reorienta- tion, does not the looming presence of injustice, inequity, poverty, and disease merit *some* attention?

America would be a better place if Dreher's crunchy conservatism won out, I'm sure. But not good enough, and maybe not even that good for very long, in our fallen, shadowy, expiring times. For both "liberal- ism" and "conservatism" are traditions with a shelf life. They are time- sensitive, and their time is out. It's not that nothing of worth remains within them—quite the contrary, as Dreher's book attests. But the modern era that called these political traditions into being—and that they, indeed, helped create—has defeated them. At this late date, being "conservative" is an inadequate ideal for humans to aspire to—as is being "liberal." What our moment requires instead is a politics more deeply human, more truly radical, something both old and new, a moral vision that might teach us anew what any healthy family, church, neighbor- hood, or nation already knows: how to conserve and liberate at once.

Two sources out of our past come to mind for help in learning to aim for this vital tension. In the American vein, the populist tradition has much to teach any who seek to nest sacrifice and justice within a broadly sacramental understanding of life. Check out Christopher Lasch's magnificent 1991 rendering of American populism in *The True and Only Heaven: Progress and Its Critics*, or track down *Tinseltown*, Pierce Pettis's folk album of the same year. Dig up a few of William Jennings Bryan's speeches. Dip into anything by the writer and farmer Wendell Berry. Each of these voices whispers persuasively that popu- lism's vitality is just a movement away.

Dreher nods toward that other, more deeply Western source when in his final chapter he points us to St. Benedict, who in an earlier age helped keep alive "the light of knowledge, of faith, of virtue, through centuries of chaos and despair." But with the same hope and for the same reason we might also look to the early Franciscans. With their devo- tion to radical charity and self-abandon, Francis and his band sought, in Chesterton's marvelous phrase, "to astonish and awaken the world." And awaken it they did—one lasting sign of which is what Chesterton calls the "Catholic Democratic" tradition, so crucial to the story of the West.

If the awakening and renewal Dreher longs for is to occur in our midst, it will surely be because somewhere some people dared to embody a moral vision deeply sacramental and sacrificial at once. It will not be because they chose to be, simply, "liberals" or "conservatives."

—2006

Kentucky on My Mind

WE DROVE INTO LEXINGTON hoping to find Kentucky, but got America instead. True, at first sight of the lush horse pastures and their handsome white fences I did start to belt out "Run for the Roses." But singing prompted me to turn on the radio, where to my dismay I detected nary a trace of Kentucky—just clipped cool voices from nowhere spitting out insipid song titles, advertisements, and traffic reports. Britney Spears's navel was all the rage there too, by the way, fitting symbol of a people that dissolves the particular into the universal: navel gazing of all varieties invariably follows.

We were anxious to find Kentucky, the real Kentucky, having already driven some 400 miles that day from our home on the north side of Pittsburgh. Following the Ohio River south along old and empty Route Seven we passed through such towns as Gallipolis, once a French settlement, and Marietta, which seemed to sprout out of nowhere; in siege-like fashion Ponderosa, Blockbuster, Wal-Mart and company encircled each, assaulting history with deadly aim. When we finally set up camp that night at My Old Kentucky Home State Park in Bardstown we at last got to hear some Kentucky voices. The old fellow in charge of the campground gave evidence, through voice and conversation, that the notion of place was still alive somewhere: he told my wife he was keeping track of all of the different states the campers were from. When Pennsylvania makes available for its residents license plates that feature (1) a tiger prowling in a dense jungle ("Save Wild Animals"!) and (2) a locomotive roaring across a darkened landscape ("Preserve Our Heritage"!) you know the concept of state-as-place is dead. I felt no compulsion to bring this decent soul into the century.

The Pittsburgher Stephen Foster wrote "My Old Kentucky Home," Kentucky's state song, while visiting relatives in Bardstown. He vividly if sentimentally captured, as the Pennsylvania Dutch would put it, an "olden" sensibility that knew place to be integral to the well-being of the soul, although already in Foster's time many Americans were sensing that time and place were falling apart. The plantation that inspired Foster lives on as a state park, complete with a golf course and the stately old mansion, which we toured. The eighteen-year-old guide, with goofy white sneakers ballooning out beneath her hoop dress, could, alas, answer few questions outside of her memorized script. She even confessed that although she had lived in Bardstown her entire life she had never gone to see *Stephen Foster: The Musical,* performed nightly for more than forty summers in the park's amphitheater. We did. The show certainly beckoned us back to another time, even if the sanitized story line and the fact that most of it was (ironically) set in Pittsburgh did much to diminish its local appeal.

We were running out of time. A Glenn Campbell song from one of my dad's old eight-tracks kept running through my mind: "The bluegrass is fine/Kentucky's on my mind." That was the problem: Kentucky was on my mind, but I was having trouble, now that I was there, actually seeing it.[1] We passed several bourbon distilleries, the sweet pungent scent drifting out of huge white wooden storage barns. Was this Kentucky? We seemed to be getting closer—the pride the folk at Maker's Mark took in their bourbon was obviously charged by local, long-term connections. A stop by Louisville's Churchill Downs also let some of Kentucky loose; this tour guide was a straight-shooting, horse-loving, Derby-proud woman. There was something palpably other there. We bought t-shirts.

Thomas Merton, the Trappist monk so widely read in the 1950s, made his home in central Kentucky, at the Abbey of Gethsamani, the oldest abbey in America. Could it be, I wondered, that this Roman band preserves Kentucky as well as any other collection of natives? When I walked into the visitor's center the monk at the desk was warmly discussing with a friend *Men Are from Mars, Women Are from Venus*—not too hopeful a sign. But I learned there that Gethsemani's monks sustain their mission by selling their own chocolates and fruitcakes, made with Kentucky bourbon. Tilling the soil, ministering the word, they wrap

---

1. Seven years after I wrote this essay my wife and I took a trip to Nashville, where I purchased a CD release of this Glen Campbell album. It turns out that Campbell was actually proclaiming that "Kentucky *owns* my mind." How many essays, poems, and stories have similar mistakes to thank for their existence?

their universal gospel in local garments, swaddling clothes with a decidedly Kentuckian look. Accent intact.

We drove through Port Royal, Kentucky, on the way home, the town from which the farmer and writer Wendell Berry famously hails. Berry, the most winsome American voice for the virtue, yea, the necessity, of community, kinship, and the human scale in general, writes eloquently and tenderly about this place. My wife snapped my picture by the post office sign. That was enough for me. Britney, I imagine, wouldn't be impressed with Port Royal, but I got a rise out of it. Still, home a few weeks now, I can't get another set of lyrics out of my mind, the raging words of singer-songwriter Pierce Pettis:

> Global village idiots
> The young and the rest
> Taking the place of the human race
> In this land I love the best

Dark thoughts. But if America does plunder the land through and through, at least we won't have to spend all that money on vacations.

—2000

Wisdom for the Recovery of Local Culture

IF THE AD HOC term "postmodern" means anything, it has to do with the breaking of the long-fraying bonds that for better and for worse have tied Westerners together, whether as towns and cities, as intellectual communities, as ethnic groups, as nations, or even as "genders." Great centripetal powers have, often with our own cooperation, had their way with us, and we know it. We find ourselves searching for something that seems lost. We find ourselves remembering less and less what it was that we lost. Even the idea of lostness has become problematic: we find ourselves doubting that anyone or thing can truly *be* lost.

Often this longing for a world more tightly bound finds expression in calls for a return to "community." Strangely, even as we issue these calls we tend to glory in the very means by which real communities—families, neighborhoods, towns, colleges, churches, businesses—have been dramatically weakened. A short list of the dissolvers might, with some argument, include: the great modern technologies, from the car to the Internet, that have made possible an unprecedented disconnecting (in the name of enhanced connecting); corporations, which have refashioned our world with these technologies; scientistic language, replacing and subsuming older understandings of nature and obligation; national organizations of various types, with their commitments to dictating the shape of and direction of the local institutions they (ostensibly) serve; and a national government, providing, in the name of liberal democracy, the political framework and ballast for all of these developments.

Whatever the causes, it's now evident that the post–World War II fantasy of a nation of interchangeable parts, in which all "individuals" are, as Southwest Airlines would have it, "free to move about the country," has turned us into a mere collection of parts, held together by little more than economic and personal convenience—not the most fulfilling or noble of social ends. Human relations of all kinds prosper only by fidelity: fidelity to kin, to neighborhood, to church, to country. We have made betraying these loyalties a way of life.

The past fifty years have left many in the mood to do some rebuilding, to take up the hard, unglamorous, but necessary work of building with integrity, from the soul outward. If national institutions of almost all sorts have abandoned their responsibility to nourish us, we know that we need to fix our gaze at the local and start again. Put one way, this vision might be termed *decentralist*: it attempts to decrease the dependence of human communities upon national organizations and structures. Put positively, the term *localist* is useful: it seeks to direct our energies toward the strengthening of those institutions that we ourselves, as face-to-face communities, have the ability to own and shape.

Fortunately for those committed to enacting this localist way of life, much of great value from the last century, despite its often ruinous record, remains to build upon. Contained in this treasury are the voices of three shrewd, perceptive observers of that century, critics who neither fantasized about a bliss-filled premodern world nor prostrated their minds before the claims of "progress." Each was critical of the world industrial capitalism made but none embraced the moral anarchy and metaphysical blindness that so many other critics of capitalism did. Most heartening, these critics, Christopher Lasch, Wendell Berry, and C. S. Lewis, achieved a broad and at times deep resonance. They struck, and still strike, chords. This makes grappling with their work a worthy starting point for those trying to think about how to recover local culture in our time.

Christopher Lasch (1932–1994), one of the most prominent American social critics and public intellectuals of the last third of the twentieth century, had by the time of his death authored eleven books and hundreds of essays and articles, which appeared regularly in venues ranging from *Harper's* and *The New York Review of Books* to *The New Oxford Review* and *Salmagundi*. A somewhat idiosyncratic socialist in the 1960s and 70s, Lasch gradually in the 80s moved toward what he, in his profound 1991 volume *The True and Only Heaven: Progress and*

Its Critics, termed "the populist tradition." Populism was, he thought, a way of seeing and living centered on a high estimation of loyalty, an understanding and embrace of human and ecological "limits," and what he termed a deep and sustaining "respect for workmanship."

Lasch's maternal grandfather managed a grain elevator in turn-of-the-century Nebraska, and also worked as a local and state politician; if Lasch was a little late for Populism proper, he surely bore its imprint long after its rather abrupt passage from the political scene in the mid-1890s. Lasch's father, a newspaper editor, worked for the *Omaha World-Herald* in the early part of his career, a newspaper which had in the previous century been edited by the Great Commoner himself, William Jennings Bryan. True to form, Lasch, as a socialist in 1969, called for a "a drastic scaling down of institutions," stressing the imperative to "combine planning with as much regional and local control as possible." He understood as well as anyone that work is at the center of the social crisis brought on by industrial capitalism, and that this crisis can achieve no resolution apart from addressing "the degradation of work," as he put it. In a retrospective piece published in 1991 he recalled how he had come to see that "The authority conferred by a calling, with all its moral and spiritual overtones, could hardly flourish in a society in which the practice of a calling had given way to a particular vicious kind of careerism, symbolized unmistakably, in the eighties, by the rise of the yuppie." For Lasch, like populists a century before him, rebuilt communities, structured by a more equitable distribution of property and laws that protect the integrity of both the earth and its families, would be comprised of people working in behalf of one another—not massive, faceless concentrations of power in the form of political and economic organizations.

Lasch's most famous calls for these sorts of communities came in the late 1970s, when he made his brilliant, bracing defense of the traditional family in *Haven in a Heartless World* and then savaged the *Culture of Narcissism* two years later. These books won him some celebrity, many adversaries, and a prominent perch as a national seer. Much to the frustration of his critics and many of his boosters, though, Lasch spoke most easily in these years in the critical rather than constructive voice. He proved to be much more adept at showing how deplorable the absence of "community" was rather than at suggesting how it might actually be achieved.

His penchant for pathology is not surprising when one considers his debt to Freud and Marx. These men and their followers tended to see diagnosis as itself a form of correction, overestimating the relationship between analysis and health. As a young scholar Lasch embraced as hardily as any this way of seeing, what he termed in 1969 the "rationalist tradition," confident in its ability to make sense of the world, to guide it toward the "rational" outworking of its own *telos*.

Such rationalism, ironically, ended up militating against the realization of his political and social ideals. It was inadequate, above all, because it did not yield for him a satisfactory understanding of that which he knew, somewhat intuitively, he was *for*. His conservative views on the family and sexuality, and beneath that his political hope itself, seemed to require something beyond science, with its pure analytic gaze, in order to be sustained. Analysis, he was sensing more fully, does not community make.

It was with great delight that Lasch in the early 80s read Alasdair MacIntyre's *After Virtue*, with its historically and philosophically rich notion of "tradition." Here was a way to speak *for* a particular way of life. Slowly he began to move toward an embrace of a sort of post-Christian Calvinism, a theological tradition that he understood to have sustained the more narrowly political "populist tradition" he attempted to rehabilitate in *The True and Only Heaven*. That community requires that a people be bound together not in a world of their own making but rather in a given world was a conclusion Lasch seemed to be slowly working toward by his death in 1994.

The question Lasch's work raises for us, then, is, can community cohere apart from a shared apprehension of and submission to an overarching spiritual reality? Put differently, can a deeply rooted social coherence obtain when the common framework is a rationalist one? Lasch had begun to think not.

Wendell Berry never fell prey to rationalist assumptions about community; from the outset his thought was touched with a religious aura. Born into a northern Kentucky farming family and community in 1934, Berry struck out in the 1950s as a young poet, novelist, and college professor, teaching in the early 60s at New York University. But in 1964

he returned home to Kentucky, taking an appointment at the University
of Kentucky and purchasing a farm in the neighborhood where he had
been raised; he became the fifth generation on his mother's side of the
family to farm in that county. His writings broadened to include not
just poetry and fiction but also essays on politics and culture, written
from an agrarian point of view that echoed earlier writers such as Al-
len Tate and Liberty Hyde Bailey. He later stopped teaching in order to
devote himself more fully to farming and writing.

As Lasch in the 60s was gravitating toward Marx, Freud, and
friends, Berry was encountering the sensibilities and assumptions that
would awaken the "green" movements of the last third of the century.
His organicism, strict and dusky in those years, reflected the conviction
that the questions raised by our presence on the planet require a turning toward ontology. The questions he was asking, he acknowledged
in an early essay, were "religious": "They are religious because they are
asked at the limit of what I know; they acknowledge mystery and honor
its presence in the creation; they are spoken in reverence for the order
and grace that I see, and that I trust beyond my power to see."

Unlike Lasch, whose parents were, in his own description, "mili-
tant secularists," Berry was negotiating the Christian faith as one who
had been reared in a family and a local culture that was church-going.
Having established early on his intellectual independence from Christian orthodoxy and its ecclesiastical forms, he moved back toward them,
and began in the 80s to sound distinctively Christian notes. His 1983
essay "Two Economies" beautifully captured the way in which he had
come to see a just political economy as rooted in the Creator's vibrant
affection toward his creation. "The kingdom of God," or as he put it in
a more "culturally neutral term," the "Great Economy," was the place
where the fall of every sparrow is accounted for, and in which all that
is made is intended for the pleasure of God; this notion of a God who
takes pleasure in his creation became a touchstone for him. Given our
subordinate place within the Great Economy, Berry contended, our own
political economy must find its proper scale and pattern by measuring
itself against the mysterious but immanent ways of the kingdom of God.

Berry's understanding of the relation between the Creator, the
earth, and its creatures had become by the 1980s searching and profound, full of the sort of harmonic vision that made Lasch's worldview
seem flat, if complex, in comparison. Berry's starting point, in one of

his formulations, was that the world is not something to be learned *about*, as the rationalists would have it, but rather something to be learned *from*. The fitting stance for the doer is one of respectful submission to a grandeur that infinitely surpasses our understanding and that must above all elicit our gratitude. Submitting in this manner to our Creator, our political sensibilities are enlivened: we find ourselves standing before one another on common ground, caught up together in the symphonic wholeness that brings both Creator and creature such delight, and working together for our mutual nourishment and for his continued pleasure.

If the ontological thinness of Lasch's social vision diminished its power, his Calvinist sensibilities at least protected him from one of Berry's tendencies: an overly hopeful estimation of the fallen human condition. It is not that Berry did not allow for a "fall" or that he did not believe in the hideous reality of evil. Rather, his pursuit of a fugitive wholeness tended to steer him away from coming to understand selfhood as what Lasch in the mid-80s described as "the inescapable awareness of man's contradictory place in the natural order of things." The tilt of Berry's thinking went against the extremity of this sort of premise; Berry at times seemed to suggest that by submitting to nature's healing graces humans may gain the ability to undo whatever harm their deviance may have caused; for him, nature itself seemed to possess redemptive power. Lasch, on the other hand, by the 1980s reacted skeptically toward those who posited the possibility of final resolutions of any sort. If Berry tended to spawn his localist, decentralizing vision in the name of organic completion, Lasch opted to ground his in a call for fundamental decency.

The difference between the two is the difference between shalom and justice, between kingdom come and this present darkness. Surely both elements, the ideal and the real, are necessary for any adequate political vision. If we fail to grasp and grapple with our creational parameters, we lose sight of our nature and destination. At the same time, if we fail to acknowledge our corrupt estate, we lose our capacity for wise and shrewd judgment about what is possible and necessary. Discerning how to weigh the ideal and the real, and how to temper one against the other is, of course, the perennially bedeviling challenge.

For the most part, it was a challenge C. S. Lewis did not bother to take up, and so to include him in this threesome seems like a category error. As Gilbert Meilaender notes, Lewis "offers no alternative program for society, for he doubts whether radical change would be, on the whole, beneficial." Perhaps had Lewis lived to see our day he would have changed his opinion on the matter. The fact is, though, that he did not insist that industrial society move in decentralist directions, as both Berry and Lasch did.

But if Lewis was not a decentralist politically, he surely was one ideally. To read his Narnia books is to enter a world of the localist/decentralist imagination. Here cities are absent and in their stead one beholds "a rich, lovely plain full of woods and waters and cornfields," with inhabitants who glory in dances, feasts, and tournaments that go on and on completely apart from bourgeois considerations of punctuality and industry. Narnians belong to one another even as they belong to their shared land, the beauty of which is itself ennobling and enriching of all that takes place within it. The loyalty its inhabitants feel for their homeland is rooted, crucially, in their mutual affection and connection to it *as land*.

Here Lewis and Berry seem to meet in full embrace, for even when rendering heaven itself Berry tends to depict it not as the transcendent other but as the final completion of the cherished, earthly place. At the end of his novel *Remembering*, for instance, when the main character goes on a brief Dantean journey from hell to heaven, it is his own hometown, the town of Port William, in its completed paradisal form, that he witnesses. Heaven, here, is the perfection of the local.

This points to a central motif in Berry's vision: connections above or beyond the local seldom nourish the local, except by protecting it from malign external influences and powers. Accordingly, at their best his heroes direct their focus toward the local, content to give themselves to discrete, democratic communities, communities that offer the possibility of the sort of "membership" (as Berry often puts it) that is their hope of health and wholeness.

This is a strict localism, to be sure, and in our globalist day a strong immediate attraction to it comes easily for many. Berry's rendering of the life of Jayber Crow, in his novel by the same name, astounds in its beauty; it is perhaps his most powerful rendering yet of his vision. Jayber, a smart young man with some time under his belt as a student at the University of Kentucky, begins to ponder anew his lowly rural origins, and is stunned to discover that, in his words, "Far from rising above them, I was longing to sink into them . . ." So he goes home to Port William and finds a hard-fought contentment, affection, and, most important, "membership" there as the town barber and gravedigger. Once more, the local is the locus of hope; the world beyond it the threat to the realization of that hope.

So in both Lewis' Narnia and Berry's Port William the respective inhabitants fiercely love their native place and feel little yearning to be elsewhere. When, in the last book of Lewis's series, the old Narnia is destroyed, its loyal inhabitants discover, to their great joy, that, as one character puts it, "All of the old Narnia that mattered, all the dear creatures, have been drawn into the real Narnia . . ." Lewis and Berry knew that as creatures we were made for places, for it is places that make us. To make us placeless is to deform us; to ground us in a place is to move us toward completion.

And yet Lewis's decentralism includes at least one element that is almost entirely absent in Berry's: the reality of social and political spheres that both transcend and nourish the local. Berry's vision of wholeness contains little place for interconnecting, hierarchical, enfolding levels of mutual good will and sustenance. He does not, in other words, seem to imagine what Lewis so richly and continually perceived: the presence of *kingdom* as a valid social form. Lewis does not stop with the democratic circle of local membership, as does Berry. For Lewis, there is something politically larger than us of which we are a part and in which we long to take part—not in ways that disrupt the local but in ways that enhance it, that nourish it, that give it a necessary reference point, that enfold it and complete it. In the Narnia series, all of this is captured, both actually and symbolically, in the character of Aslan, whose business—one might say calling—is to protect and help prosper the local, even as he moves in and out of it in the name of a higher order. Lewis's understanding of "membership" transcends the local, yet at the same time makes the local *more* local, for it helps it to understand itself in relation to the ultimate referent.

The ultimate referent is, in the end, integral for helping us to find our way beyond our severely fractured condition. If Lasch goads us into remembering what civic decency requires, and Berry captures for us the creaturely estate that is our birthright, Lewis confirms for us the necessity of participation in a kingdom, in a social form that links us to that which is beyond even as it nourishes us where we live. Those decentralists who despise on principle the social forms that transcend their particular communities will be fated to watch as their own children are lured away by that which lies beyond the particular place they know. The answer is not to reject the universal for the particular, or the particular for the universal, but rather to understand and enact the proper relation of the one to the other.

Which brings to mind the relation of not just the particular to the universal but also the relation of our present to our future—a sobering consideration in our recklessly cosmopolitan age. At their best, though, these writers provide evidence that hopeful eyes, eyes that see history with a comic vision, will give localists their best chance of being not merely heard but heeded. Lasch in his last books dismissed "progress" and embraced instead hope and justice. Berry taught us about heaven through the eyes of a gravedigger. Lewis wrote of triumphal last battles even as he warned of devils, witches, and evil enchantments. They each came to see that the goodness that, finally, governs this world manifests itself most fully in the concrete, particular realities of local life. It is with this premise that successful calls for community in our time will begin.

—2002

Take Me Home

THE PENN STATE UNIVERSITY geographer Wilbur Zelinsky believes something exists called the "Pennsylvania Culture Area." Last month I found it.

I was home in Bedford for spring break, mooching off Mom, Dad, and my grandmother, just like old times. My kids were at my wife's parents. My wife and our dog stayed home. True, I got a lot less sleep during this stay than I used to a couple of decades back. And I had to lug along a satchel full of student papers to grade. But for a couple of days I was a lone son, spoiled by attention, much of it in the form of food.

My grandmother, age eighty-two, got up the first morning I was there and, pushing aside a distressing level of bodily hindrances, began to prepare herself for the day's main event: the monthly potluck dinner of the Bedford Valley Senior Citizens. I could go as her special guest, she said, doubting I would accept the offer. It took me about five seconds to realize it was an offer I couldn't refuse. Zelinsky's Pennsylvania Culture Area (PCA) was beckoning.

After half a semester's immersion in the history of Pennsylvania with a bright, inquisitive class of fifteen, mainly Pennsylvanians, this was just the field trip I was primed for. We'd learned about cultural landscapes, traced Indian-colonial relations, studied Civil War editorials, and read folklore from the Alleghenies. Zelinsky maintains that Pennsylvania is the locus of one of only three "major colonial culture hearths of the Atlantic Seaboard." But unlike denizens of the other two hearths—southern New England and the South's Chesapeake Bay region—Pennsylvanians, he says, "remain oddly oblivious to the particularity of their turf."

I know them well. I number myself among them. I attended first and second grade in the (now closed) red brick schoolhouse less than a mile from the township building where we went for the potluck dinner. Later my family moved from the western part of the PCA to its eastern side, landing in Lancaster. For the past decade I've taught in Beaver Falls, in the Pennsylvanian west. I've long loved the state as a homeland. I just didn't know much about it.

So I decided to take a break this semester from the big macro-themed courses I usually teach to think small, to *feel* small, to bring history into closer contact with place—my place. This dinner I was attending as both student and neighbor.

I dropped my parents and grandmother at the door, parked the car, and walked in to find my mom scurrying around helping to get food set out and my dad mixing it up with old friends. Voices boomed across five or six lines of narrow tables. After ten minutes or so a retired Methodist minister stood up to offer a blessing; my mom told me he and his wife drive in each month from Harrisburg—a two-hour drive—just for the dinner. Within a few minutes someone had brought a tray filled with food for my grandmother while others stood in line; a lady came by passing out homemade Easter candy.

I loved the meatloaf, which a man serving as treasurer had made—two pans worth. I couldn't resist Grandma's deviled eggs, and the chocolate cake with the cherry icing absolutely hit the spot. My dad was shouting the news of his recent retirement down the table to his cousin Shirley when the president, a gruff, beloved man, recently widowed, called the meeting to order. The minutes were carefully read. Happy birthdays were sung. All rose to pledge the flag. Bantering and badgering ensued on the financial state of the organization. ("So you want a big trip? Where do *you* think we're gonna come up with the money?")

About an hour in the entertainment was introduced: Floyd and Roger, plucking and strumming guitars, both superb. They sang together and urged everyone to join in. Nearly everyone did, including me, childhood songs rushing back with a force as sweet as the voice of the lady behind me, who seemed to feel a particularly keen yearning for the peace in the valley one song promised. Some were longing to fly away, to be sure, while others, like my grandmother, were more peacefully present, living testaments of the virtue of life lived on the sunny side.

Toward the end I found myself staring out the window at the state flag, with its deep dark blue, its proud horses, its glittering gold. I know where I'm retiring, I had joked, the spread of homemade delicacies in view. But of course few of these friends and neighbors will be around then. Will my generation of Pennsylvanians have enough culture to keep this one going? Will this circle be unbroken?

—2010

EDUCATION

Babel-On

The News from Lake Woe

14 April 2006
Good Friday

My Dear Screwtape,

A happy V-Day to you, old friend. I'm just back from the CCCU's[1] thirtieth anniversary bash—urr, "convention." But was it ever a bash for us! While the exhilaration lingers I wanted to file this update. Then it's off to the evening's festivities, with fantastic tales to tell.

I can think of no better way to put it, Screwtape, than to say that Babel-On has become a spectacle, hellish comedy in high form. After three days of collective giddiness (along with those assigned to attend, many of our associates chose to take vacation there) I fear we may need to take action to keep our confidence in check. But that is more of a disciplinary concern than anything, Screwtape, because, at the risk of sounding obsequious, your brainchild has become a self-perpetuating success, sure to keep rolling along in devastating fashion for years on end (or, more precisely, *until* the end). I'll jot down some of my observations, though I'm sure you'll have anticipated each. But the devil is, after all, in the details—and so the delight!

Pure and simple, our lingua franca has become the parlance of this sector of the Enemy's realm. Witness: even our trainees at the conference, on hand mainly to learn *their* language, found themselves understanding so much of what was going on that their supervisors are

1. Council of Christian Colleges and Universities —ed.

scurrying to find another site for future training sessions. The mantras, of course, were amusingly chanted, as always. ("Integration!" "Faith and Learning!" "Christian Scholarship!") But deep and serious exchanges in their own tongue were rare, confined to the occasional threesome commiserating in a bar outside of the hotel somewhere, so cynically self-absorbed they pose no threat at all. Yes, their silly old dream of a widely shared Christian grammar is history.

Which is to say that the academic disciplines are thriving among them. Our Know-Nothing epistemology is continuing to flower and bloom in unexpectedly useful varieties. When the evangelicals meet by discipline in their own "Christian" societies, their collective fervency is so amusingly *sweet*, as they unabashedly grope for blessing and promotion within the grand professional fiefdoms—a yearning, I might add, that we have intensified by playing on their isolation from the circuits of professional power. In short, the CCCUers are not only seeing through their disciplinary frameworks—they are *feeling* through them as well. You begin to sense the full measure of our glee!

When they do come together for larger, collective purposes, like this convention, the only groupspeak they know, increasingly, is that which the university itself uses to remain intact: Christian ethics-lite. If their disciplines provide the CCCUers with a means to communicate with fellow historians, psychologists, engineers, etc., the academy (!) provides them with an increasingly common tongue—and their accents are by now practically undetectable, perhaps the most heartening indicator of our recent gains. At occasions such as this conference they find themselves in a bedeviling quandary. They sense that the cacophony of their interfacing disciplines is potentially disruptive, so in order to achieve some semblance of unity (it is, after all, a "council") they resort to that lovely combination of sentimental pieties and misguided ideals that intertwine to keep the university itself churning forward. Foucault, Pocock, Gramsci, Chomsky, Douglas, Bloom, Gilligan, Hawking, Lacan, Wilson, and company could never survive a conference together, at least when made present through this variety of proxy, and so these wannabes end up resorting to whatever ethical crusades we've got charging through the academy just to give themselves at least some sense of purpose and direction. At this convention we witnessed a baptizing of the academy's pieties so energetic and sincere it makes John himself look like an underachiever.

I can hear you cackling, Screwtape. Read on. At this particular gathering the Diversity Charge was serving as the social glue of choice. One particularly ardent moralist went so far as to exhort her colleagues to "crush the tyranny of the c.v.!" (yes, churlish revolutionist tones and all!) and make "Diversity" the aim and end of hiring! Hell's bells, it was a blessed moment! They are actually beginning to buy Diversity as an *epistemological solution*, a way to give their colleges (and "universities"—ha!) a more consequential role in the Enemy's realm. My respect for your vision grows deeper by the week, O Shrewd One. We have now effectively shielded their eyes from seeing that the language, the only language, that could possibly assimilate Gramsci, Derrida, and friends into their own enterprise is only in the most distant of ways connected to that pious blather that we, quite successfully, have termed "evangelicalism." (If only Luther could see all of this—he'd bolt back to the monastery in a heartbeat!) And it is precisely their self-conscious "evangelicalism" that will keep them from seeing the obvious, salient fact: that "diversity" without a deeply unifying grammar, studied intensively and spoken easily by all, leads to, ahem, just more diversity, with all of its delicious fruits. Yes, old boy, the banquet we are spreading before us is growing richer and richer. If we continue to divert them from gaining a genuine knowledge of their own tongue (with the usual time-honored tactics: huge teaching loads, accreditation requirements, professional aspirations, committee work, intradenominational anarchy, doctrinalism, and so on) they don't stand a chance of glimpsing that common vision that could turn "diversity" into a real weapon, enabling the Enemy to infuse his power more fully into their efforts.

I shudder to ponder that possibility. But trust me, Screwtape, they are a *long* way from that sort of dangerous movement, and the gap is widening all the time. Carl Henry is no doubt turning over in his recently dug grave. Those particularly dangerous Enemy seers—MacIntyre, Milbank, Hauerwas, let alone Augustine, Aquinas, and Edwards—seldom make it out of the "Bible Departments," if they even make appearances there. Even that old fool Lewis is becoming less and less harmful, as the evangelicals clutch at him as an icon rather than as an example of what they might become. So successful have we been in divorcing theology from "spirituality" that even if one of these CCCU academics were to crack open an Edwards or a Hauerwas they would no doubt find the texts impenetrable—or, better yet, uninteresting!

I could go on and on, but you get the picture. They are, truly, just babbling on, happy to be on their merry evangelical-professional ways, conditioned as they've become to the rewards that therein lie and reduced, unwittingly, to either the most pragmatic or the most sentimental of binding ties. They oscillate between a collective mushiness and a hard-headed "realism" that grasps for some means, any means, to maintain their continued *raison d'être*. And it's only this most holy union of American pragmatism and evangelical sentimentality that keeps them from simply dissolving into the blessed state of nature the academy itself is fast becoming, the Hobbesian holy war of all against all.

You may by now find yourself asking, how far are they from what they would perceive as catastrophe? The break is indeed near, but so dim have they become I doubt there is any chance of their detecting it. We never forget your rallying cry: "Misplaced Hope!" And so we continue to feed them enticements that they, in their soppy American way, find irresistible: not just Diversity, but Technology! Outcomes! Community service! Distance Learning! Assessment!—anything to keep those touchingly naïve hopes burning. We'll keep them busy trying to keep themselves intact under the illusion that they're actually pushing *us* back—the very definition of farce!

They are, at present, so harmless that we might as well keep them around for the near future rather than allowing them to disintegrate, if for no other reason than for their exquisite entertainment value. There's nothing quite so amusing as a follower of the Enemy who thinks she's accomplishing something when she's not. Their continual quiet preening at the convention gave rise to frequent and riotous fits of hilarity— as if articles in "professional journals" were moving the tectonic plates themselves! They decry their own "enclave" tendencies with earnest, unctuous handwringing, while failing to see that the real enclave (so pivotal for our purposes) is that of their own location in the professional class! The thrill it gave me to see how much they actually *despise* the communities in which they live—hankering like moon-eyed adolescents for Berkeley, Cambridge, Oxford, Manhattan—is well nigh indescribable. Their condescension? Almost enviable. They mouth "Christ Transforming Culture" rhetoric while snootily turning aside from the only real "cultures" (you were *on* the day you came up with that splendid little piece of jargon, old boy) they will ever really have a chance to "transform." Fortunately, they can't see that, in the words of one of their own shrewdest observers, one can be "regional without being provincial." As you might guess, they dismiss him as near kin to the Amish. Such obtuseness, in the name of the Enemy himself, is truly what makes our work so rewarding—and our victory so certain.

Yes, this crowd, and the millions they represent (if *these* are their best and brightest, may their kind increase!) are much more than harmless. Their usefulness to us, in fact, is steadily on the rise. The "students" they produce, after four years of that welter of "theory," "method," and schlocky piety are excellent fodder for The Economy—not to mention effective builders of it. After such conditioning what else could they be? Their high levels of cognitive congestion, coupled with their sappy and shallow sense of identity and purpose, blinds them to the Final Solution. Not surprisingly, they can't see the most obvious fact of all: that as the earth goes, so goes the race. Slightly more remarkable is the fact that most of their own leaders are actually embracing the Final Solution as their own, going so far as to dignify it with euphemisms like "globalization"! (They fancy themselves "realists"—how right they are!) Order itself will soon be dissolved like so much styrofoam in fire. Triumph is at hand!

You are no doubt wondering if *all* is sweetness and light. I could point to a few troubling nuisances—the fact, for instance, that some CCCU colleges have begun to welcome Catholics and Orthodox into their numbers—irksome because these lonely souls at least have live communal recourse to the tradition of their realm. And, yes, the loudmouths from Grand Rapids continue to spout off, although I think we've so diverted their attention from their own realm that they're often beyond earshot of their own potential followers. Many of the "Reformed" big shots don't even bother to attend the conferences of the CCCU-related professional societies (attending such a conference would, happily, feel embarrassing to most of them). The departures of these "stars" into the "real" academy actually works to our advantage because it perpetuates the subtle, commonly believed (if not actually spoken) lie that it's in "the academy" that the real action is happening. And of course once their stars make it to the academy our homogenizing and fragmenting pressures begin to do their work with even more success.

In fine, Screwtape, the level of danger has never been lower. In my judgment, we have eliminated this threat. The CCCUers are babbling on to Babylon, as planned. In fact, I am pleased to report that we are able to reduce the number of our associates in these districts even beyond what you requested, freeing a larger numbers of them to move into more needy areas. It is truly a day for jubilation, dear friend. We continue to stand at allegiance, inspired by your example and nourished by your large and looming presence. I shall lift a toast to you tonight, for I remain,

Yours Truly,
Blyvyn

—2001

Sights Unseen

Why Theology Matters Most

The educated classes, unable to escape the burden of sophistication, might envy the naïve faiths of the past; they might even envy the classes that continued unthinkingly to observe traditional faiths in the twentieth century, not yet having been exposed to the wintry blasts of modern critical thinking. They could not trade places with the unenlightened masses, however, any more than they could return to the past. Once the critical habit of mind had been fully assimilated, no one who understood its implications could find any refuge or resting place in premodern systems of thought and belief. It was this experience of disillusionment, more than anything else, that was held to distinguish the artist and the intellectual from the unreflective creatures of convention . . .

—CHRISTOPHER LASCH, "The Soul of Man under Secularism" (1994)

Language is at the heart of the problem. To profess, after all, is "to confess before"—to confess, I assume, before all who live within the neighborhood or under the influence of the confessor. But to confess before one's neighbors and clients in a language that few of them can understand is not to confess at all. The specialized professional language is thus not merely a contradiction in terms; it is a cheat and a hiding place; it may, indeed, be an ambush. At the very root of the idea of a profession and professorship is the imperative to speak plainly in the common tongue.

—WENDELL BERRY, "The Loss of the University" (1984)

Historical Prologue

IF IT MEANS ANYTHING to be modern, it means to be done with theology. Once, long ago, theology was the linguistic mortar that kept the creaky edifice of Christendom intact. But the most radical architects of the modern order understood all too well that if you could get at theology the rest would tumble—walls, ceiling, roofing, even the fundament itself left to crack, crash, and burn. They went to work, with spectacular success. As our very own Thomas Jefferson was urging his nephew to "Fix reason firmly in her seat," and to "Read the Bible . . . as you would read Livy or Tacitus," Thomas Paine was stridently declaiming to the Western world his own new and improved dogmatics: "I do not believe in the creed professed by the Jewish Church, by the Roman Church, by the Greek Church, by the Turkish Church, by the Protestant Church, nor by any church that I know of," he proclaimed in *The Age of Reason*. "My own mind is my own church." Just a few years later, at the turn of the nineteenth century, Frederich Schleiermacher tepidly suggested that Jesus Christ was "distinguished from all others by the constant power of his God-consciousness, which was a real being of God in him"; religion, proposed Schleiermacher, amounted to a "perspective and a feeling," a "sense and taste for the infinite"—this from a book entitled *On Religion: Speeches to Its Cultured Despisers*. Orthodox theology, in the Protestant vein, was in trouble.

America's progress toward this new rationalist faith was, as you might expect of a province, a bit slow—but only a bit. By the 1880s Princeton Seminary, the last major Protestant seminary not to invite the theological liberals in, was hunkered down in a full-blown defensive posture, with B. B. Warfield and A. A. Hodge slinging grenades with what can only be called, with affection, Presbyterian panache. By the third decade of the twentieth century Princeton's remaining anti-modernist scholar, J. Gresham Machen, was forced to depart and launch his own seminary, which became Westminster Theological Seminary. The situation worsened. In the 1930s, when as a recent convert Kenneth Kantzer (who would go on to become a theology professor at Wheaton College and dean of Trinity Evangelical Divinity School as well as editor of *Christianity Today*) was looking for a theologically conservative seminary he remembers his options as three, all tiny and fledgling: Westminster, Faith Theological Seminary (which had split from Westminster), and Dallas Theological Seminary. Kantzer recalls the outstanding scholarly achievement of conservative American evangelicals in that lean decade to be Wilbur Smith's *Therefore Stand*, a very basic defense of orthodox Christian faith. Smith's highest degree was a *high school diploma.*

Say hello to the world the moderns made. "Modernity" has popularly, and with sophistication, been explained as the product of various "forces," a litany with which we are all familiar: industrialization, capitalism, urbanization, high-tech communication, and so on. Well and good—so long as we keep in mind the brute fact that *people*, people with minds and hearts and wills, were driving those revolutions. And some of the most brilliant of these revolutionaries were those who made the destruction of Protestant theology their aim. They nearly succeeded.[1]

Their task was not purely destructive, though; in fact, they understood themselves primarily to be builders: of new schools, new cities, new nations—of a whole new world. First and foremost, they knew they needed to build a home: a place to lay their heads, to entertain guests, to train their progeny. Soon the great patriarchs of the modern epoch—Darwin, Hegel, Herder, Comte, Marx—found themselves living on in digs that were posh by any standard. The modern university, in this scheme, would provide the intellectual might and the raw manpower that would transform the world, remaking the landscapes of the earth and soul to match the rationalistic blueprint that was their guide and their hope.

In mid-nineteenth-century Britain an unusually astute theologian named John Henry Newman had the acuity of vision to see what was coming —and it did not look much like the revolutionaries' glorious, grandiose architectural renderings. The diabolical reality, perceived Newman, was that as theology was disappearing so was the hope of

---

1. I thank Dave Guthrie for pointing out the Oliver Stone-esque quality of this spin on the destruction of Christendom. True: the depiction of the rise of modernity in the preceding paragraphs does underscore the self-consciously revolutionary dimension of the story at the expense of the more ironic, unintentionally secularizing side of it. (For that side see, for instance, Marsden, *The Soul of the American University*, and James Turner, *Without God, Without Creed.*) Still, the Voltaires, Jeffersons, Paines, and other intellectual heavyweights were out to take Christendom down, and they saw orthodox theology as the chief enemy. The more moderate, unintentional secularizers were to a significant degree responding to the enormous amount of cultural and intellectual pressure being placed upon them to abandon the (orthodox) ship by the radicals whom I here highlight.

unity of any kind—political, ecclesiastical, cultural, intellectual. For in theology's place was emerging the clamoring welter of academic "disciplines," each intending to lay claim to the sacred throne from which theology had been deposed. Cut loose from theology, Newman predicted, the disciplines would each gain a certain epistemic autonomy. Then they would battle it out for the right to rule. George Marsden, in his sprightly and subversive *The Soul of the American University: From Established Religion to Established Unbelief*, captures Newman's critique of the nascent Protestant universities well: "In place of unity . . . each of the special sciences would emerge with its particular angle of vision for which it would claim universality. . . . Under Protestant auspices universities were likely to emerge as a conglomeration of special sciences, united most by their common resolve to be free from each other and any external authority."

Here we are. Viva Postmodernity.

The Mexican writer Octavio Paz describes *pachucos*, a Spanish word used in the 1950s for Mexican teenagers living in American cities, as being distinguished by a "furtive, restless air," ashamed both of their Mexican origins and of their inability to become authentically American. They have "long since left their homeland," Paz writes, and "can hardly speak the language of their forebears." The "secret roots, those that connect a man with his culture, have almost withered away." It's a striking portrait, at least to me, for when I see American Christian academics, I see *pachucos*: homeless souls living with more than a little strain and shame.

We are a curious sight. Modern intellectuals and premodern believers at once, we are both the children of the damned and the children of the blessed (and just who are the damned who are the blessed depends on which precinct you happen at the moment to be inhabiting). We were mainly reared in Christian environs, and we have the accent, when we're not dissembling, to prove it. We know that "Be Thou My Vision" is not an Elizabethan love song. We've winced at hearing ourselves utter "Amen!" when some classmate in a grad school seminar made a pleasing point. We are, either by birth or by naturalization, other.

Yet we are not simply, to refer to Lasch's observation in the epigraph, "unreflective creatures of convention"—not even to moderns. We ventured bravely into their realm, the mighty graduate schools of the university, to seek our fortunes and earn our fame, and perhaps even to advance Christ's fame. We have been schooled in and stamped by two settings that represent two different kingdoms, kingdoms that speak different (if somewhat converging) tongues. We are, to varying degrees, bilingual.

This brute social reality—our mixed birthright—is disorienting for those who claim citizenship in another land. We continually run the risk of tarrying so long in Babylon that we, unlike the recent Jewish arrivals, gradually forget the songs of our own land, failing to feel anymore the impulse to sit down and weep for home. We have emerged from the university changed. We've learned new hymns and creeds; we've learned to speak a new language—that's what our credentialing required, after all. But more than we care to admit or see, we have forgotten (not so much as individuals but rather as a collective whole) our native tongue, the backwoods talk, the language of the country cousins back home—the "fundamentalists."

The time is right, after these past fifty years of evangelical higher learning's rapid and spectacular ascent, for a stern and penetrating season of self-examination. And at this particular moment an inward look is especially appropriate, for the master language that replaced theology, the language of Reason, has itself collapsed and eroded. We, often with a sigh, call this linguistic fracturing "postmodernism." But, as Marsden and others suggest, perhaps it should be with a shout. For if as Wendell Berry argued in 1984 "language is at the heart of the problem" in the university due to the emergence of the "specialized professional language," then the "common tongue" he claims we need is in our possession: the language of theology, the one-time unifier of the common life. If in Christ all things consist, and if Christ himself is the Word—the *logos*—then we Christians have hope: deep, abiding hope in the final unity of knowledge and culture. An embrace of an essentially theological vision, rooted in a profound immersion in Christian language, promises to help us put our fragmenting communities of learning back together again.

Devilish irony: at the precise moment that a convincing command of this tongue is most urgently needed, we evangelical academics are stuttering and stammering, sometimes reduced, pathetically, to hand gestures. Like children of immigrants, we can make out the conversation, nodding our heads, but gone is our fluency: the ability to own a language and create with it. The truth is that we, bona fide denizens of the academy, tend more easily and comfortably to think in the language of our disciplines; it's there, after all, that we have done our most serious and sustained thinking. If we're honest, we're not exactly sure what to do with theology, as our misguided notions of it reveal: Sometimes we assume it to be the province of specialists, on whose turf we seldom dare to encroach (would anyone but a "theologian" read Aquinas?). Or we see theology as "literature" (think *The Divine Comedy*). Or we construe it to be mainly the study of dogma (supralapsarianism, anyone?). By these ways and others we tend to undercut its primary, most true essence: theology as above all *language:* a wonderfully mysterious and complex and alive form of thought that enables us to see, to hear, to discern, to inquire, to render, to draw near.

Sadly, we who are trying to do higher education "Christianly" find ourselves in a state not unlike the Mexican woman visiting Berkeley who wrote back to a friend in Mexico, "Yes, it's very lovely, but I don't belong here. Even the birds speak English. How can I enjoy a flower if I don't know its right name, its English name, the name that has fused with its colors and petals, the name that's the same thing as the flower? If I say *bugambilia* to you, you think of the bougainvillaea vines you've seen in your own village, with their purple, liturgical flowers, climbing around an ash tree or hanging from a wall in the afternoon sunlight. They're a part of your being, your culture. They're what you remember long after you've seemed to forget them. It's very lovely here, but it isn't mine . . ."

Like her, we sense that there is so much to see and explain and underscore and revile, including the subject matter of our own "disciplines." But without a deep theological fluency we can't seem to pull it off. The venerable ideal of the integration of faith and learning requires the most searing and searching of theological visions. But how can something as profound as the "integration of faith and learning" possibly take place if the would-be integrator possesses no deep knowledge of the Christian tongue? Like the Mexican woman in Berkeley, we find ourselves at a loss. We sense that important sights are going unseen, both to our own loss and to the loss of our community. We open our mouths to speak, and nothing comes out—at least not what we sense *should* come out.

The time is right for a recovery of our tongue. And who better to do it than us, Christians who are trained and paid to study and think? Should we neglect theology, should we continue to default to the Babel-esque cacophony of the academy, we will perpetuate the betrayal of Christ's kingdom and contribute further to the decimation of Christian culture. We really have but one choice: to immerse ourselves vigorously in the deep pools of recorded Christian consciousness left for us by that great cloud of witnesses. We must seek this saturation not so much for dogmatic delineation (a necessary if not sufficient part of the theological task) but for visual orientation: to learn how to *see*. We *will* see. The question is, which language will we allow to train our vision?.

It is good to be reminded that much is at stake. The great and grandiose social project the purveyors of modern Knowledge hoped to construct has turned out to be, at its best, a "Kuwaiti bazaar" of lifestyles, as Richard Rorty puts it. Whether one sees this consumerist playland as an angelic triumph or a devilish terror, we can at least all agree that whatever the (post)modern world has turned out to be, it is not the Kingdom. And it is to build the other City that we Christians, speaking our native tongue, are left on earth to do: we are to begin the rebuilding of the world, a foretaste now, to be culminated later.

We have the means to do so. Theologian Stanley Grenz reminds us how and why. Christian theology, he avers, "sets forth more completely the nature of community that all religious belief systems in their own understanding seek to foster." Christian theology, Grenz contends, provides "the best transcendent basis for the human ideal of life-in-relationship, for it looks to the divine life as a plurality-in-unity as the basis for understanding what it means to be human persons-in-community."

I take it that Christian colleges are set apart as institutions for the purpose of becoming embodiments of such communities, particular instantiations of the Kingdom of Christ. And if the perspective I have here sketched is at all on target, then our crises of identity may well be linked to the larger problem of the fragmenting of the common language and culture that has so disrupted the academy in recent decades. It is this academy from which we have all proceeded, carriers, ironically, of the very virus that is our foe. But we have an antidote, one that promises to return us to health. That antidote is a collective immersion in our common tongue.

How might this vision be enacted?

How about chapel speakers who challenge not just the students, but the entire college, speaking thoughtful, winsome Christian language?

Why not a "Christian Thought" lecture series every year, in which we welcome the Grenzs, Vanhoozers, Wells, and Siders to campus—not primarily for the students, but the faculty?

Reading circles? What might happen if reading groups labored through Alasdair MacIntyre's *After Virtue* over the course of a summer? How about Aquinas?

What could we do in terms of curriculum? Might we develop a core Christian history and theology course in which faculty from every department take part by leading discussions of Augustine, Bonaventure, Luther, Newman, Barth, Hauerwas?

In sum, I contend that our problems with identity stem not from our failure to "agree" on particular theological points but rather from our inability to speak a common tongue. We must make the recovery of this tongue the primary institutional focus—of faculty, of administrators, of students. I, for one, would rather see students—and faculty—leave our colleges speaking fluently as Christians, complete with a wonderfully winsome accent, rather than proclaiming a "worldview." Which would you rather have over for dinner?

We need to think Christianly. We need to *see* Christianly. And we need to make it our chief task to build profoundly Christian communities of learning. This requires that we be on a first-name basis with our own great Christian intellectual forebears—not so that we might become "cultured," but so that we might become Christian.

Do I hear an amen?

—2001

Liberalism's Lonely Triumph

I WAS STARTING THE second year of a PhD program in U.S. history at the University of Delaware when the professor who would direct my dissertation, Guy Alchon, dropped a remarkable book into my mailbox: Christopher Shannon's *Conspicuous Criticism: Tradition, the Individual, and Culture in American Social Thought, from Veblen to Mills,* published that year (1996) by Johns Hopkins University Press. In brief but powerful fashion it gave me the best glimpse I had yet had of what it might mean for a historian to do "Christian scholarship." Just as important, it spawned a vision of the modern world that in the years since I've not been able to brush aside.

Guy called it a "dark" book and thought it would resonate with me. (I'm almost sure that was a compliment.) The semester before I had taken his seminar on "The Political Economy of American Intellectuals" and had written a paper he had liked quite a bit on the American social critic and historian Christopher Lasch. I ended up expanding that paper into a biographical study of Lasch's life and thought in my dissertation, but only with considerable help from Shannon's work.

It turns out that as an undergraduate Shannon had been a student of Lasch's at the University of Rochester and had remained close to him until his death from cancer in 1994; in the midst of his illness Lasch had even read and commented on Shannon's manuscript. Such proximity to Lasch, though, did not stop Shannon, as he brought his argument to a close, from a vigorous few pages of criticism of his former teacher. After spending 180 pages dissecting modernity's secular, rationalist frame of mind, he turned to the example of Christopher Lasch to underscore his overarching point: Americans were trapped in a political and cultural straitjacket due to their complicity in modernity's "critical project of uprooting all received traditions."

Shannon tagged this project "the tradition of conspicuous criticism," and attempted to locate Lasch within it. "More than any other intellectual since the 1950s," Shannon wrote, "Lasch carried on the struggle with modernity as it took shape in the tradition of conspicuous criticism." But for all his acuity of vision, Lasch seemed unable to accept one central, ominous historical reality: due to the modern rejection of a world governed by a "spiritual order" and the affirmation instead of "the creation of value and meaning by autonomous human subjects," the sort of community for which Lasch and so many others—left, center, right—yearned was impossible. Whatever their own self-flattering perceptions, Americans were, constitutionally, "a people bound together only by a belief in their inalienable right not to be bound together to anything." Given this brute philosophic and political reality, the unceasing jeremiads pronounced by moralists like Lasch, however morally alert, were doomed to fail. "Calls for moral responsibility are pointless apart from some context of shared values, and the only values Americans share are the procedural norms of a libertarian social order, the thinness of which incite the anxiety that drives the jeremiad in the first place." He concluded the book with a damning pronouncement: "The bourgeois attempt to construct a rational alternative to tradition has failed."

In its opening pages Shannon had disclosed that he was a Catholic, and his cool, gutsy diagnosis of what he termed "the Reformation-Enlightenment attack on tradition" revealed the remarkable extent to which he was willing to foreground his faith even when writing as a young vulnerable scholar. I found myself cheering for him with every turn of the page. I later learned from a mutual friend the cost of his theological affirmations: he had been unable to land a tenure-track teaching job, his Yale PhD and enviable publishing record notwithstanding. My friend's sense was that Shannon's intelligent, self-conscious Catholicism had helped do him in.

It was Shannon's position as a Christian writing within the academy—indeed, *Conspicuous Criticism* began as his dissertation—that helped account for my own grateful and enthusiastic reception of his book. I suspected, as I made my way through it, that Shannon felt as uncomfortable in the modern American university as I did, and his book seemed at least in part an effort to probe the roots of his dis-ease and then explain his findings to his (uncomprehending) peers and professors. What was provoking Shannon (and me), in short, wasn't simply a wrongheaded "worldview," or some other species of philosophic abstraction. Rather, it was a way of life that was doing the provoking—the actual living out by real people of this "rational alternative to tradition," which Shannon palpably despised. By the century's end this way of life was reflected in its most perfect progressive form within the American university, where both he and I, as fledgling Christian scholars, found ourselves uneasily living and moving and having our being.

It's easy enough to point out the most obvious, non-Christian features of this university-sanctioned-and-sustained way of life—the common understandings of marriage and sexuality, for instance, and the accompanying commitment to quarantine any who would speak against the received wisdom. Wading into the university, though, I discovered that the idealistic language of liberation seemed to provide cover for lives that often were considerably less than hope-filled. One of my classmates was about to be married, and I remember hearing another student wisecrack to him about the divorce that was sure to follow—a barren, ugly cynicism, rooted, sadly, in an all-too-intimate knowledge of the empirical evidence.

It's no wonder that in this atmosphere so many of my peers turned to the study of history for hope. Here again, though (and consistent with Shannon's thesis), most of their research endeavors had to do with some attempt to discover who was oppressing whom, and what sorts of liberation the oppressed were being denied, whether due to law, custom, or belief. Fair enough—I was in no way resisting the importance of gaining as full a historical understanding as possible of any variety of oppression. But did these folk really think the larger, well-traveled narrative about "oppression" and "freedom" really captured the whole story? Was there nothing else to write besides the ritualistically rehashed liberation tale?

No. This was among the saddest conclusions I came to during graduate school. For most of my peers, I realized, there was no other story. The other possibilities—philosophical, ideological, theological —had long been ruled out, debunked and filed under the "oppressor" category in the long, continuing history of freedom's triumph. No wonder a Christopher Shannon couldn't find a job—a quick glance at the introduction to his book provided a startling self-portrait: this was no scholar. This was a two-headed beast, a dragon of the sort assumed to have been slain long ago by liberating crusaders.

Well, if you can't kill it, you can at least send it yelping back to its cave.

As it turns out, the culture wars framework I've here employed, this us-versus-them, Christians-versus-secularists idiom reflects only one side of the story of the modern university—an important side, but not the only side. More subtly apparent is the uncomfortable reality that beneath the sometimes obvious dissimilarities in worldview and way of life lies an uncannily similar self.

It was Lasch's keen perception of the nature of this newly emerging self that had helped attract me to his work before I had started my studies at Delaware. His improbable best-seller of 1979, *The Culture of Narcissism: American Life in an Age of Diminishing Expectations*, both summed up and deepened a mounting conviction shared by many that Americans were changing in fundamental ways: becoming less able and willing to practice citizenship and exchanging the common life for, as he put it, "purely personal preoccupations." In this book Lasch tied this historical shift in character to the ongoing advance of liberal capitalism, with its ever-colonizing market and ever-expanding state. "The atrophy of older traditions of self-help has eroded everyday competence, in one area after another, and has made the individual dependent on the state, the corporation, and other bureaucracies," he noted with sharp disdain. "Narcissism represents the psychological dimension of this dependence."

It was a powerful argument. It was also precisely the type of argument—a jeremiad—that Shannon found at once understandable, monotonous, and hopeless. For him, the ending of the American story was already scripted; a collective turning, somehow, away from corporate capitalism wouldn't remove the fact that America's deepest (and sole) point of unity was, as modernity played itself out, the notion of the liberated individual—a laughably weak foundation upon which to construct anything like a "commonwealth" or a "republic" or even a "community."

Shannon's pessimism about the possibility of truly improving our common life resonated with my experience: whether Catholic, Protestant, or irreligious, our common circumstance as academics by the 1990s seemed indeed to be a post-communal one. Creatures of our age, we had finally emerged as that most sorry of things: humans in mere skeletal form, starving for a fullness, a socially embodied richness, that prevailing civilizational patterns and our own moral commitments (both chosen and inherited) precluded us from achieving. The paeans to "freedom" rang out with regularity, but within me (and, I gathered, within many others in varying degrees and ways) they effected mainly a mild sense of desolation. Everyone seemed to be trying a little too hard to celebrate liberalism's lonely triumph.

A sure sign of our loneliness: the near total absence of any genuine political discussion or debate within the university, whether in graduate seminars, public lectures, or less formal settings. All graduate students "knew," to take the most obvious and telling example, that "conservatism" (rarely defined or actually discussed) was pathological, and so hideous and dangerous; this assumption ended up setting the ground rules for any consideration of "conservatism" as either a historical subject or a point of view that might fruitfully be brought to bear on our discussions of authors, politics, or life.

My gut sense was that the culture of the university, truth be told, didn't have the strength or stomach to accommodate any serious challenge to the dominant liberal point of view anyway, a truth the university's boosters could never imagine, let alone consider. Jean Bethke Elshtain's remark about the particular kind of self that has accompanied what she, echoing Phillip Rieff, calls "the triumph of the therapeutic culture" comes to mind: it is, she says, a "quivering sentimental self that gets uncomfortable very quickly, because this self has to feel good about itself all the time. Such selves do not make good arguments, they validate one another." The university in the nineties seemed a case study of this self's triumph: genuine, principled argument could rarely muster the strength to make even a cameo appearance there. We had by then become a people fighting mainly *for ourselves*—a posture that fosters, with rapidity, a defensive state of mind, not one centered on intellect, rationality, open-mindedness, and all of the other attributes academics ascribe so easily to themselves.

Elshtain's perspective on this peculiarly disabled modern self resembles and is in fact indebted to Lasch's; indeed, she and Lasch were close companions in the last decade or so of his life. But Lasch, writing in the 1970s from within a self-consciously rationalist framework, could at that point only employ explanations rooted in social and economic causes for what he knew to be true about us; absent was the metaphysical, philosophic dimension that would enrich his work in the eighties and nineties. Behind this shift in his thinking lay the remarkable work of an author Lasch read with enthusiasm in the early eighties: Alasdair MacIntyre, perhaps the dominant moral philosopher of the last third of the twentieth century.

MacIntyre had famously moved from Marxism to Thomism by the 1981 publication of the controversial, pathbreaking *After Virtue*, in which he presented an interpretation of the modern self that both echoed and deepened Lasch's (and others') depiction of our enlarging cultural narcissism. On MacIntyre's view, moderns, having gradually abandoned the long-dominant Aristotelian tradition of virtue ethics, had devolved into emotivists, assuming as a matter of course that "all moral judgments are *nothing but* expressions of preference, expressions of attitude or feeling, insofar as they are moral or evaluative in character." "We live in a specifically emotivist culture," contended MacIntyre, one that locates moral order not in a benevolent, overarching *telos* but solely within the individual self.

Like Lasch, MacIntyre looked at the twentieth century and saw chaos, fractures and fragments of a moral order that were hopelessly, willfully strewn about the wilderness of the West. "Each moral agent now spoke unconstrained by the externalities of divine law, natural teleology, or hierarchical authority; but why should anyone else now listen to him?" he sensibly asked. Also like Lasch, he made it clear that he was not one more ex-lefty who had made a home on the right: capitalism, for him, was deeply implicated in this whole destructive macro-historical turn. The tradition for which and within which he was arguing, he emphasized, "is at variance with central features of the modern economic order and more especially its individualism, its acquisitiveness and its elevation of the values of the market to a central social place." Those Reaganites reading him in the eighties could find only selective solace in his critique of the secular modern order.

After Virtue was much debated and discussed, from the academic seminar to the popular press (at least in England). In my case, it was MacIntyre's discussion of the modern self *over against what it might look like* that had the deepest effect. Lasch and Shannon had helped me to see more starkly the plight of the individual in the jaws of modern capitalist civilization, but neither had provided much by way of normative guidance. Here MacIntyre spoke powerfully. From the perspective of the Aristotelian-Thomist tradition, moderns, he believed, had "suffered a deprivation, a stripping away of qualities that were once believed to belong to the self." The typically modern self possessed "a certain abstract and ghostly character," disconnected as it was from that which was to define it: "In many pre-modern, traditional societies it is through his or her membership in a variety of social groups that the individual identifies himself or herself and is identified by others. I am brother, cousin, and grandson, member of this household, that village, this tribe." For MacIntyre, there was no escaping this elemental identity. "I am born with a past; and to try to cut myself off from that past, in the individualist mode, is to deform my present relationships," a form of amputation with costly spiritual and social effects. "These are not characteristics that belong to human beings accidentally, to be stripped away in order to discover 'the real me'"; in reality, there was no such thing as the isolated, autonomous, independent "individual." In fact, MacIntyre dubbed the "individual" "that newly invented social institution."

This vision of human obligation, identity, and community clearly had no place in the contemporary university. If, the writer and scientist Wes Jackson has quipped, the university today offers one single major—upward mobility—then its central function, aged platitudes aside, is to provide functionaries for that mighty tandem, the corporate economy and state. The graduates of the modern university, accordingly, leave it (and the whole American educational system) in no philosophic or moral condition to embrace an identity centered on service to kin or place. The university trains us to serve other masters.

MacIntyre's understanding of the self cast long-awaited light on all sorts of perplexities, from the failures of "conservatism" and "radicalism" alike to the struggle I was having to reconcile my own university-sponsored "upward mobility" with my rural, working-class roots. I could now see more clearly than ever that the sort of peace for which I yearned, a peace joining the social and personal, must include a deep fidelity to kin, to place, and, finally, to my own divinely shaped design—all of the things, in short, that modern wisdom had told me I could (and should) shuck at will. The futility of such a way of life had become apparent: to abandon an identity rooted in kinship, telos, and place would be to abandon *me*.

After Virtue was an audacious book, a heady attempt to implode, from the very center of the university itself, the mythological narrative of the West's progressive march through history. That entire academic disciplines took MacIntyre seriously is vivid testament of both his intellectual force and rhetorical verve. But if the book was quietly feisty, it was also defensive in tone and tack, a defensiveness eminently understandable, given MacIntyre's embattled stance, yet one that ended up inevitably diminishing the power of his argument.

Most damaging, perhaps, was the simple fact that MacIntyre made little provision in his narrative for the implication of the tradition he was honoring in the eventual triumph of the individualistic culture he damned. Arguably, the entire modern project, at least in its political manifestation, began as a corrective to the inhuman and subhuman features of traditional Western cultural and political structures and practices. If this is so, then those Christians who for centuries provided harbor for this vision of life ended up, tragically, failing it (and us) by not successfully enlarging the sphere of ordered freedom for all within their midst, whether the poor, women, or outsiders. It may be obvious, but it's worth stating: the philosophic tightness of MacIntyre's overarching argument against modernity did nothing to dissolve the actual historical failures of his forebears. They *invited* the great modern political, intellectual, and religious revolts. Given this failure, greater measures of sympathy and pathos plied into the narrative might have aided his efforts.

This criticism does not diminish the immensity of his achievement, of course. After MacIntyre and the many he has influenced, including Lasch, Shannon, and Elshtain, "modernity" looks less like "progress" and more like an experiment gone stupidly awry, a cultural corrective that in grand misshaping fashion has assumed control over the entire culture. "Liberating" the individual is the only end our civilization collectively knows; we barely perceive that other understandings of the common life have existed, and continue to exist, even in our own (multicultural!) midst. Today, insofar as we as a nation are one it is due to marketing, technology-spawned collective fantasies, and, paradoxically, the individualist creed itself. And insofar as we are "individuals," we become so by ritualistically cutting ourselves off from our native communities and giving ourselves over to a "freedom" that consorts with the designs of the (almost) all-powerful to exploit our aimlessness, our appetites, and our hopelessness in the ongoing creation of a "global" society. Could this truly be a satisfactory solution to the ancient question of how to hold in balance the one and the many?

George Packer's beautifully crafted memoir of 2000, *The Blood of the Liberals*, provides as poignant a personal rendering of this, our common circumstance, as anything I've recently come across; it's the book to read in tandem with *After Virtue*. The grandson of a self-proclaimed Jeffersonian congressman from Alabama and the son of a self-consciously liberal law professor (and a Stanford University provost during the late sixties), Packer tells a three-generational story that, with disarming frankness, seeks to understand what has happened to a country that seems unable to bind itself together in ways that honor its venerable, organizing ideals of citizenship. Repelled by the tendency of twentieth-century liberals like his father to cut themselves off from their own "blood" to serve the mind (he notes, for instance that his father gave the university "all his energy, much more than he gave his family, because he believed in the high importance of the life of the mind"), he narrates his own journey through his family's past, subtly entwining this personal narrative with a broader argument about the direction of American history itself. His troubled conclusion? "The main problem of our time is a loss of belief in collective self-betterment." The revolts of the sixties, he contends, may have changed many lives, but they "didn't leave behind a viable worldview," making what he calls the post-sixties "ruins of liberalism" understandable and pathetic at once. "This was the face of American prosperity at the end of the twentieth century," he acidly writes: "racially tolerant, environmentally conscious, and determined to wall itself off from the low-paid countrymen who cut its grass and wait on its table and look after its children."

Packer etches a self-portrait of a leftist longing for a community he can't find. In his mid-thirties he goes so far as to investigate his aunt's evangelical world, and even travels from his home in Boston to Washington, DC, to attend the massive 1997 Promise Keepers' rally, in search of one single experience of social, interracial solidarity. Understanding "religion" to be a "challenge" to his "liberalism," he nonetheless senses that evangelicals have that which he's been unable to locate on the left, "something that can't be summoned on demand: vitality." At the end of his evangelical explorations he wistfully concludes that "All the years of rational training at home had killed the nerves that might have been receptive to religious stimuli."

Packer was looking in the right direction—*cultus*—even if his own search ended in disappointment. The communities that will be forged in our midst will surely be religious in a self-conscious way, for actual religions—our collective responses to the mystery that lies beyond and within our seeing and touching—are what have historically made possible the sorts of communities we in our time so struggle to achieve. Communities need a religion like children need parents: apart from the ordering presence of a religion, we fly apart and die alone.

MacIntyre closed his book in cryptic fashion by commending to us as our hope not merely a "religion" but the monastery itself—a place where Christians do live and die together. "We are," he concluded, "waiting not for a Godot, but for another—doubtless very different— St. Benedict."

Seen from this point of view, Christian colleges with "mission statements" like the one at which I teach seem driven at least partly by countercultural, communal visions like MacIntyre's: we profess Christian doctrine and practice as our defining features and our primary driving force. But a walk to the campus bookstore, or a visit by an accrediting agency, or even the phrase "mission statement," remind me of the extent to which we at the college, despite our clear differences of belief and behavior with the secular academy, swim in one common, contaminated pool. It leads me often to wonder whether it is even possible, short of moving in far more transgressive directions than currently is our practice, to do higher education in a distinctively Christian way in this globalizing, homogenizing age. Is our own halfway covenant with modernity not heroic so much as quixotic?

I confess these doubts while working within the bounds of a community that wrestles actively (I wish more actively) with these questions. And herein lies the irony of my own quest: my deepening discovery of the human need for a life more richly communal has mainly occurred while studying and working within one of the places most responsible for the dissolution of traditional understandings of the common life: the modern university—even, all too often, in its "Christian" guises.

But perhaps there is a logic beneath the irony. Before there were places like Delaware, there were places like Harvard and Princeton and

Yale. And before there were places like Harvard and Princeton and Yale, there were places like Oxford and Paris and Wittenberg. Perhaps if true communities are to be born in our postmodern age, they will yet begin within the walls of communities like those of long ago, communities that set themselves apart in order to dedicate themselves to discovering who we are, where we are, and how we ought to comport ourselves as we walk with our Creator on this earth. This sort of collegial renewal, Benedictine in scope and end, deserves all the effort we have to give.

—2003

Centers That Hold

Twenty years ago a boy I know went off to college.[1]

It was the age of argyle knee socks and skinny ties, of spikey mullets and tidy perms—a time, in sum, when college students were trying to figure out how to be hip without being hippies. Sting and *Thriller* filled the air, *Cosby* and MTV the screen. And the genial pep of Ronald Reagan, contagious, in its way, was already making the poor guy the Democrats sent up into a sacrificial lamb, though the election was still two months away.

All of this was the stuff of mystery to this boy, the fledgling collegian. He had been overseas for several years, and had just returned home that summer. John Travolta, flowers, and transistor radios had given way to Boy George, plaid, and boom-boxes. It was all unsettling, in an exciting sort of way, and he was eager to jump in. And he was scared to jump in.

How does one safely enter something as powerful and vast as a *culture?* From the protection of the family room? Behind the wheel of a car? Inside a mall, perhaps, wandering from shop to shop?

But this way of encountering a culture makes it sound a little too abstract. There was, I assure you, *nothing* abstract about re-entering America for this young man. Not only was he trying to find his way in a country only strangely familiar, he was, by leaving the safety of home, and childhood itself, putting himself on the line—and we all know what that feels like. It's a reality show without the show, no national audience observing or hefty paycheck awaiting: just you in your cramped dorm room, attempting to "adjust," trying, while your hick

1. This essay originated as an address delivered at Geneva College's 2004 fall convocation.

Elvis-impersonating roommate is belting out off-color Conway Twitty songs, to figure out if N-I-K-E is pronounced *Nike* or *Nik-ee*.

By the time the Conway Twitty crooner came along the boy had made his American landing. He had jumped, and he was in. But he wasn't in the family room (until fall break, when he slept for more than eighteen hours his first night home, to his mother's consternation). He wasn't behind the wheel of a car (since he didn't have his license yet—he was only seventeen, and eighteen was the legal driving age in the country where he had been living). And he certainly wasn't in a mall. No, he was at a small Christian college in a semi-suburban, still largely rural part of southeastern Pennsylvania, living on something called a "campus." This was his primary entry point into that bewildering, indeed ominous-sounding world of America, 1984.

Fortunately for him, this college was a familiar place: it was his dad's alma mater—if not the mother of his father's soul then certainly its governess. His father had attended the college while the boy was in elementary school and had been a presence on campus. *Everyone* knew the boy's dad, it seemed, and many of them even remembered the boy. They ended up sharing many of the same professors; it was both impossible and completely natural that such legendary figures as Dr. Figart and Mr. Osborn were now his teachers too. He was playing on the same soccer field upon which ten years earlier he had watched the amazing Jude Nixon glide around. It was, in short, a safe place, and it was a beloved place. It was probably just the sort of place that he, at this delicate and critical moment of re-entry, needed.

But unfortunately for him and for the other members of the community, it was also a college that was struggling, and struggling at many levels. Enrollments had been low for several years. Salaries had always been low. Professors were worn down and out from years of overwork. And the cafeteria food was bad—by today's elevated standards, at least.

More deeply, it was a college that was struggling to map a course for itself in that world of 1984—a world that was not just bewildering to freshmen, but to the faculty and administration too. This was a college that had come into being fifty years earlier in response to what its founders had perceived to be serious, even tragic wrong turns other colleges and seminaries—and indeed, the entire culture—had taken in the first decades of the twentieth century. They judged these new directions to be deeply offensive to good thinking and living and injurious to the kingdom of Christ. In the midst of vast cultural and spiritual disarray, this college intended to provide reorientation and direction for Christians seeking to live faithfully in a troubled time. It was a noble aim.

But it's one thing to set out to be a college; it's another to actually achieve it. To attain to the reality of *college* is no simple task, after all; in the least, to truly be a college requires that the educational community in question possess both social integrity—people living together as they should—and intellectual integrity—people thinking together as they should. By taking upon itself the holy responsibility of instructing human beings in living and thinking, a college community publicly obligates itself to enact those high ideals for which it stands in all aspects of its life: from the way it structures its pay scale to the way it structures its classrooms; from the attention it gives to students to the attention it gives to food preparation. If it fails at discerning the nature of the good life or at integrating this understanding into its own life, it will not possess integrity and will look ridiculous—indeed, will be deserving of ridicule. The social and intellectual spheres must come together to form one philosophic, ethical, aesthetic whole—this is what the ideal of *college* means, and teaches—and if the community in question actually comes to embody the most central and elemental human ideals, college is achieved: the name fits.

As you might suspect, the particular college community the boy found himself in was filled with earnest, smart people striving to attain to this highly demanding ideal. But their confusion and disorientation were palpable, even to freshmen: Confusion about what it means to live as a Christian. Confusion about what it means to live as an American *and* as a Christian. Confusion about the ideas emanating from the broader academy. Confusion about the direction the world was moving. And confusion about its own vocation within the church and the world. Both its social and its intellectual integrity, in short, were under threat. It was struggling to overcome a profound if elusive sense of disorientation. And it was not alone.

Because, as it turns out, this sort of pervasive and fundamental confusion about who humans are and how we should live was, arguably, the defining quality of the entire twentieth century, a quality whose era-shaping hold persists into our own day as well. *What Are People For?* is the title of one book I've assigned in classes, and the very need to ask that question aloud gives some sense of the dimensions of the

cultural and political crisis that frames our everyday life. Older understandings of human beings, and history, and time, and God, have in the
past two hundred years been cast aside, with no small amounts of relief
and conceit. But the century that those living one hundred years ago
expected to deliver us to the Promised Land, to the New Jerusalem, and
beyond, turned out mainly to leave us who survived it asking, fearfully,
confusedly, this one enormous question: *Who*, after all, *are we?* In the
aftermath of a century that featured political brutality of cataclysmic
proportions, that saw what was perhaps the most culturally, intellectu-
ally, and economically sophisticated nation in the West seek to destroy
the Jewish people, that has seen a gaudy and transient form of wealth
triumph only at outrageous cost to the earth and its creatures, we cry
out, with tears bitter and hot, what are people *for?* What is our purpose?
Is there anything worth fighting for? What is worth *living* for?

Our disoriented college freshman, attending this disoriented little
college, found himself looking for answers to these questions, as they
emerged inchoately from his soul and worked their way into his mind.
He found some professors who had serious ideas about the shape of
the present. He found others who were more concerned to preserve
a sense of the world that was passing. In this second category was Dr.
Joan Tompkins, a great and passionate student of English literature, the
advisor of the drama club to which he belonged, and one of the college's
most infectious, demanding, and fiercely wholehearted teachers. One
fall he took her course called Major English Writers, and found himself
lugging around a massive tome. In time he discovered that this volume,
The Norton Anthology of English Literature: Great Authors Edition, contained many searching, learned meditations on all of these questions
regarding the nature of the civilization, and the age, and the even more
fundamental matter of human identity. One of these meditations took
the form of a poem that begins like this:

> Turning and turning in the widening gyre
> The falcon cannot hear the falconer;
> Things fall apart; the center cannot hold;
> Mere anarchy is loosed upon the world,
> The blood-dimmed tide is loosed, and everywhere
> The ceremony of innocence is drowned;
> The best lack all conviction, while the worst
> Are full of passionate intensity.

This poem, William Butler Yeats's "The Second Coming," written in the darkening years that followed World War I, stands among the most famed of the thousands of attempts to capture in concentrated form the nature of our times. *Things fall apart; the center cannot hold* . . . *Things fall apart; the center cannot hold* . . . *Things fall apart; the center cannot hold* . . . This one line has become embedded in our souls like a chant over these eighty years because it reflects, I take it, both the reality of our deeply fallen estate and our current civilizational circumstance. For a brief glance backward reminds us, again, that we have not always regarded our situation in such a dire fashion. In the eyes of many of our nineteenth-century forebears, the center was not just holding but growing ever stronger, as the deity of Progress, with dazzling pillars of fire and cloud, led the nations forward. Things were falling together, not apart; triumphally—if not always merrily—we went along.

But things changed. The shock of discovering that history might actually have been moving in a quite unbelievably different direction, palpable in Yeats's poem, registered vividly in the mind of the American social critic Lewis Mumford, who years later put it this way:

> We all had a sense that we were on the verge of translation into a new world, a quite magical translation, in which the best hopes of the American Revolution, the French Revolution, and the Industrial Revolution would all be simultaneously fulfilled. The First World War battered and shattered those hopes, but it took years before the messages received through our eyes or felt at our fingers' ends were effectively conveyed to our brains and could be decoded: for long those ominous messages simply did not make sense. Until well into the 1930s we could always see the bright side of the darkest cloud. We did not, while the spirit of our confident years worked in us, guess that the sun upon which we counted might soon be in eclipse.

Little that has happened since World War I—whether the terrifying things like global depression, Hiroshima, and the Cold War, or the dazzling things like television, smart bombs, and the World Wide Web—has served to strengthen the center to which Yeats referred; quite the opposite, in fact. Those traditions that had helped to construct that center—including varying forms of Christian belief and practice—had lost their shaping power, and the search was on to fill the vacuum they left. By the mid-twentieth century the West was in the final stages of the long and slow process of shifting for whatever cohesion it still required to another center, to what we might call, simply, a *self-center*: not a polity founded upon a broad (if unstable) consensus about a deity who creates and commands, but instead a polity devoted most fundamentally to a self that deserves and demands.

Put differently, we—Americans and others in the West—have chosen, or perhaps defaulted to, not one transcendent center but rather to millions of human centers, each self a law until his- or her-self. Once our old binding agent lost its hold, *we* fell apart. And apart we remain.

We have tended, in a hopeful but fuzzy way, to call our new estate "freedom." And indeed, in the course of this long-coming fracturing we have, true to the odd and eminently unpredictable way in which history moves, made political and cultural gains that have led to an enlarged sphere of true freedom. With our heightened perception of the self have come various movements and laws that have won vital protections and liberties for those who had been systematically marginalized and oppressed due to gender, race, or ethnicity.

But paradoxically, these gains have been made possible at least in part by this vast cultural and social fragmentation, and the bonds that we-the-liberated have grasped hold of to tie our little self-centers together are not so impressive. Usually when we-the-liberated wish to feel a sense of belonging to some person or group we end up looking for the code and symbols of those who are part of our own self-selected, generation-driven market niche and follow distantly along, being sure to reserve the right to leave (whether a job, church, town, or marriage) at a moment's notice, and so protect our "freedom." Sadly, this form of belonging is a faint shadow of the sort of thick membership that words like "commonwealth" and "neighborhood" and "family" and "tribe" and "church" and "college" describe and demand. Our more shallow way of connecting cannot, and does not, hold. Inevitably, we, disconnected and distant, find ourselves looking inside again to face once more that lonely, looming question: What am I *for*? Just "good times"? "Fun"? "Pleasure"? "Work"? "Success"? "Me"?

We're not just disoriented—we're barren. We don't know to whom or to what we belong, or should belong. In Aristotle's useful way of framing it, we know neither our formal end nor our final end. We awaken and find that we have jumped into a culture moving at breakneck speed, powered by great economic forces dedicated to expanding and servicing the appetites of the voraciously hungry selves we've become, and we eat and eat and eat and we're just as hungry as before, so we eat and eat and eat . . . and we're still hungry. Still empty. Still alone. And we realize that we have become, as we see in flashes of dark honesty, tiny centers, the tiniest centers imaginable. And these tiny centers *are not holding*.

Like our bewildered collegian of two decades past, *we need help*. We need safe places, beloved places, vital places, places whose integrity teaches us who we are and how we, in these strange times, should live— and, perhaps most crucially, how we can become a "we."

And so one day we, like that freshman, find ourselves sitting in an academic convocation at the start of a new year. And against all odds a moment of insight occurs: perhaps colleges might actually exist for this one thing: not to train students for "careers," not to provide fun or "culture" or even an improved vocabulary, but rather to help us, post-modern pilgrims that we are, to gain the rooting—spiritual, intellectual, moral—that we with every fiber of our souls long for, and that might aid the transformation of the lonely and hollow selves we've become into the robust and rich people God has called us out of darkness to be.

And what of the old Christian West? Maybe it was time for it to go. Like a college, a civilization that fails to incarnate the ideals it has champrioned deserves, if not ridicule, at least a stern rebuke and a sober exit. Maybe instead of fighting so hard to preserve a dying civilization we should allow the most noble ideals of our Western heritage to call into existence a new people, one that more faithfully adheres to that ancient, timeless vision of the good life, a people that will begin this time with a markedly improved awareness of the worth of each particular creature of God, and, indeed, of the inestimable worth of the entire creation.

Perhaps this people's intense and passionate conviction will call multitudes back to their Maker, as ceremonies of innocence and justice and peace forge new centers: centers that hold.

—2004

Language Unlocked

In *The First Year Out: Understanding American Teens after High School,* Tim Clydesdale, a sociologist, pulled off an enviable authorial feat: he came up with a metaphor that carried his book.

Which in turn carried eleven faculty members at my college into several charged hours of discussion. As part of a recent faculty development initiative we gathered for three mornings of conversation, using as our centering text Clydesdale's already much-discussed 2007 study. Although disciplinarily diverse, with departmental representation ranging from communications to biology to athletics, we held in common an unsettling combination of receding memories of our own first years out and ample, often bewildering experience as teachers with Clydesdale's generational cohort.

Clydesdale, with a winning combination of disciplinary reticence and professional provocation, had already put a few of us on edge by the time we arrived for day one, including me. Those of us with significant teaching responsibilities in our core curriculum were, we had read, inveterate practitioners of, in Clydesdale's all too memorable phrase, "liberal arts hazing," the touchingly misguided attempt to get Meaning into the Lives of Our Youth. This description would cover, I presume, the team-taught course to which half of my load is devoted, Invitation to the Humanities, which includes units on death, love, and the 1960s. By Clydesdale's lights, we're nuts.

Why? His reading of a munificence of surveys, interviews, and theoretical studies leaves him contending that first-year college students are decidedly uninterested in grand adventures of most kinds beyond the social. In the first year out, he concludes—and here's where he turns to his metaphor—college students stash their souls away in an "identity lockbox." They devote their main energies not to discovering the world of the academy but rather to surviving the world of the campus—and the two, seemingly, have little connection. "High school graduates do not set out to 'experience the world' or find their unique role in it," he explains. "Their focus is intensely and almost exclusively personal," centered on "daily life management." Clydesdale's report is clear and stark: "Except for a handful of teens who become the future intelligentsia . . . the overwhelming majority of teens I studied appeared culturally inoculated against intellectual curiosity and creative engagement."

As Vonnegut might put it: strong stuff. What's a humanities prof to do when confronted with, in another of Clydesdale's disturbing phrases, the students' "discourse of nonchalance"?

Clydesdale urges us to lie low, radically recalibrate our expectations, and hope for some pedagogical openings in years two and three. Given his framework and data, it's an altogether reasonable conclusion. It is also a counsel of despair. Rather than accepting it, we might first give Clydesdale's own discourse a closer look. It may provide some insight into the general recalcitrance toward educational exploration that Clydesdale finds so pervasive.

The First Year Out is scrupulously social-scientific, guild sociology at its best. The students' encounters with sex, alcohol, and drugs Clydesdale classifies under the rubric of "managing gratifications." Students do this "managing" while "navigating relationships," though "meaningful connections" are often lacking. These varied activities reflect our "American culture's socialization processes," which "generate a large proportion of relatively diligent workers" who are for the most shaped by "popular American moral culture"—a culture that may or may not, he thinks, provide "a sufficient basis upon which to construct independent biographies or sustain shared lives."

What is Clydesdale saying? Better, what *language* is he *speaking*? To the extent that these descriptions sound simply like plain English, it's a sign that we, too, have been "socialized" in the "popular American moral culture" he describes, and have thus learned to think (without thinking) in the lingua franca of the modern American public sphere. It's a language rooted in the passé but persisting attempt to be "value-neutral," "universal," and "objective" in observation—as if Nietzsche had never lived, Derrida had never spoken, and thousands of PhD dissertations had never been written unmasking the fraudulence of this particular language game. But the game is still being played, and played hard, arguments against it having little political effect against the forces aligned to maintain it. Meanwhile, real argument becomes impossible (you can't argue with "objectivity"), true diversity is minimized in the name of cordial and controlled obfuscation, and the corporate capitalist (dis)order, rooted in the (scientifically achieved and justified) manipulation of people, animals, and the earth, rolls right along.

To be sure, social science has developed a sophisticated language, and not without its uses. What it has proven unable to do, though, is tell anyone what is really going on—a big drawback for those would try to *teach* with it.

Is it conceivable that eighteen-year-old American college students can possibly be brought into a richer relationship with themselves and their world when guided by this tongue (in whatever its disciplinary dialect)? If, as the historian Wilfred M. McClay puts it, "the relationship to the objects under consideration is always implied by the language we use," then our turn more than a century ago to naturalistic science for the academy's master tongue has bonded us, discipline by discipline, to a way of seeing that keeps subject and object detached and so facilitates our own continuing evasion of respectful, attentive participation in the grand reality that binds us together. The question the writer and English professor Curtis White poses to environmentalists might be put to educators as well: what if, White asks, the rationalistic language of science "were actually the announcement of the defeat of what we claim to want?"

White's question underscores a basic global truth: we human beings have no choice but to make moral hay with whatever language we're tossed, regardless of its purported neutrality vis-à-vis moral questions: this is simply the way the human animal lives. To teach a new vocabulary to a people is to lead them into a new set of relationships with each other, with their past, with their institutions, and with the earth itself. What will these relationships be like? It depends at least in part on how wise the language is—how capacious its vision of reality, how intricate its sense of our circumstance. What Clydesdale's study mainly reveals, by both his research and his discussion of it, is the intellectual and moral folly of this, our modern tongue, and why our efforts to do the work of education with it have been so disappointing.

If we want to get into our students' identity lockboxes, I suggest we first break open the academy's linguistic lockbox. Fifteen years ago, in his history of the American university, George M. Marsden noted that in view of the widespread collapse of confidence in the Enlightened quest for scientific objectivity, the academy, if only for the sake of consistency, should welcome—indeed nurture—more linguistic richness, rather than construct what he dubbed the "multicultural melting pot" that in the name of diversity has actually defeated it. But it's not just the students, it seems, who wish to guard their identity lockboxes—the academy is guarding its identity, too. Should we be surprised when our students follow suit?

A generous measure of linguistic freedom, a freedom that encourages intellectual exploration at the foundational level of religious, moral, and philosophical pursuit, might not just free up some students for real discovery—it might free the academy too.

—2009

Project Babel-On: Postscript

Top Ten Tips for a Clean Sweep

1 April 2008

*As we near the completion of this project, I'm sending along some remind-
ers, lest we lose focus and take a victory lap too early. No fumbles as the
game winds down, please. Raise Hell. —Blyvyn*

10. *Don't let dreamers be leaders.* They can't be trusted: make it known.
    Dreamers apprehend possibilities beyond the status quo—*our*
    status quo. Lock them up in think tanks. Quarantine them in
    committee work. Push them into middle management. Lure them
    into writing articles, essays, books—just don't give them anything
    close to *authority*. If dreamers become the public face of Christian
    colleges and universities, they might actually raise some money—
    among other things.

9. *Spread the language of the market.* These fools using *our* language to
   explain *their* task: sublimity itself! When they describe the process
   of attracting students as "selling them on the college"; when their
   admissions counselors understand themselves to be giving "sales
   pitches"; when they refer to students as "customers": it all feeds a
   beautifully manipulative impulse, as they objectify the students, in-
   flate themselves in their own eyes, and subtly transform everyone
   from human beings into economic units. Language shapes reality:
   they of all people ought to know this, but of course they don't. Keep
   it from them, and let the music of the market play on.

8. *Screen it.* All reading and any significant forms of communicating
   must continue to be shifted to the screen. Email, PDFs, websites,

PalmPilots, blogs, blackberries, "social networks," etc., etc., etc.—these must continue to flourish, and be seen as not only necessary but, more crucially, as forms of *progress*. Thus we will continue to corrode their ability (not to say their desire) to engage in sustained arguments of any kind. The screen's ill-suitedness for real reading will continue to lead them into more desirable forms of pleasure: movies, games, pornography, etc. And their continuous emailing will only continue to erode their communities.

7. *Keep politics real.* Realpolitik, remember, is what they need to think of as politics itself. By all means keep their personal sense of identity tied to the two major political parties, and then foster the usual highly productive attitudes (i.e., snide and haughty "progressive" professors sneering at their backward, "conservative" students). By *no* means permit any sort of space for serious criticism of both parties, or of the whole system. Keep them thinking "realistically," whether about national politics or institutional politics (as they understand the one they'll understand the other).

6. *Say it with numbers.* They must continue to believe that the most comprehensive, authoritative, accurate, and necessary means of apprehending reality is through numbers. Of course, it's fine to permit them to profess belief (of a certain type) in "the Word," but when it comes to making actual decisions about personnel, about the nature of the institution, about students, they must continue to turn to numbers for the truth. A focus on "objectivity," "data," "research," "assessment": this will keep them away from the power of the word—which is, of course, the ultimate danger.

5. *Separate the many from the one.* Our biggest threats have always come when they manage to understand that their hopes for communal vitality and strength center on their ability to keep the one and the many in tension, honoring particularity even as they submit particularity to the whole. *Multiculturalism, diversity:* these are ideal ideological forms so long as they make no serious efforts to think about how these forms of particularity might find their place in the one. (This of course will serve to remind you that we must continue to steer them away from thinking about the cursed three-in-one formula as anything other than a useful but minor household product.)

4. *Bring on the consultants.* Homogeneity, homogeneity, homogenei-ty. (See preceding point). Consultants are our perhaps most useful agents for our broader aim of fostering global culture. They are the waymakers for the corporate order. For the price of looking like everyone else (they even call it "branding"—ha!) and thus staying afloat they'll drain their coffers. It is, truly, a thing of beauty.

3. *"Out-source" all conceivable operations.* This ensures that the col-lege in question will never discover its own peculiar genius, and thus attract attention through a creative articulation and embodi-ment of its own identity (again, the one-and-the-many problem). Much better to integrate multiple corporate presences into the in-stitution, each driven by explicit, unabashed monetary ends, each making significant decisions in potentially key places of commu-nal vitality: libraries, bookstores, residence halls, cafeterias, etc.

2. *Make the branches the trunk.* Or, to put it differently: strengthen the "majors"; weaken the core. The majors must be the guiding epis-temic and pedagogical avenues for the academic enterprise. If the college does seek to operationalize a "core curriculum," make sure that it's driven by the "departments," the "disciplines," or the "ma-jors" rather than by any daring attempt to work beneath them, phil-osophically or theologically, and so create the vision of a complex, finally existent whole. *Colleges exist to train professionals*—never let them forget this! So long as you do this, the colleges, regardless of their supposed affiliation, will remain what we designed them to be in the first place: training grounds for the corporate order, and thus for our own ultimate end: destruction of the so-called "kingdom."

1. *Keep the lights on.* As our research has repeatedly shown, the two conditions most likely to incline these fleshlings to pray are direct exposure to nature and to darkness. Keep the cars, planes, and trains running all night. Make sure the televisions, computers, phones, and whatever else you can dream up are always beckon-ing, summoning, demanding. And don't *ever* let them turn off their computers. As long as we keep the lights on they'll forget what they're really dependent on, redefining life all the while. "24/7"? A hellish substitute for the heavenly motto they used to mumble now and then: *pray without ceasing.*

—2006

SPORT

Why We Love Football

IT'S A WARM AND hazy day, and Frank and I are at our sons' Little League practice, watching baseball but talking football. Nothing could be more typical of Pittsburgh in June. The Pirates, at ten games below .500, are ambling toward their fifteenth straight losing season. The Steelers' training camp starts in six weeks. Hallelu.

Frank knows football, and certainly western Pennsylvania football. He is Frank Namath, the nephew of the man who some forty years ago made our town, Beaver Falls, almost a household name. When "Uncle Joey" got big, Frank tells me, his mother had to move out of the town and into a tiny house on a hill that overlooks it. Strangers from all over the place had been besieging her, gawking, poking, prodding. She, blue collar through and through, found herself suddenly the mother of an icon—presumably no easy thing. Especially here.

How do we love the Steelers? Let me count the emblems. Running on any given day through our old residential neighborhood, I see Steelers flags, camp chairs, license plates, decals, posters, mailboxes, bumper stickers, and articles of clothing—including my own t-shirt. When I, a lifelong Steelers fan who had never lived closer than three hours to Pittsburgh, came out to interview for a job, I was astonished by all of the Steelers paraphernalia—and delighted. Back home, my black-and-gold-bleeding brother-in-law (he to whom I once gave a Steelers cutting board for Christmas) referred to my landing a job in "Mecca."

How to live with all this devotion? When the Steelers made their remarkable, improbable Super Bowl run in the 2005–6 season the atmosphere across the region was electric, all day, all night, each week bringing a new level of primal voltage, powering countless parties, conversations, newscasts, even classrooms. At the college where I teach students, faculty, and staff could speak of little else, to the sometimes flamboyant annoyance of the out-of-staters in our midst. Two nettled young men, one from Ohio and the other from Cyprus, shaved their heads in protest, not of the Steelers so much as their fans. That included me, I suppose: I wore my Steelers necktie on Mondays and my replica jersey on Fridays—Black-and-Gold Day, city-wide, all month, Pittsburghers sporting their truest colors in effusive display.

January was, you might say, unusually warm that year, the temperature rising as the mercury dropped. Musicians wrote and recorded dozens of Steelers songs, some of which were played on radio stations, made available through the Internet, and danced to at clubs and bars. ("What is it about the Steelers' success that makes people say, 'Where's my kazoo?,'" quipped the *Pittsburgh Post-Gazette* columnist Gene Collier.) When at last Super Bowl Sunday arrived I was amused and charmed most by the elderly woman who into our staid two-century-old Presbyterian church wore a Steelers vest with matching ear rings, hobbling into her pew with a glimmer in her eye. How did the pastor make it through the sermon? It's hard enough under ordinary circumstances to preach to restless pew-sitters, let alone when they're wearing face paint, as the children in one family did.

Few other dimensions of our common life so totally capture the twenty-first-century American zeitgeist as the NFL. Perhaps none do.

Certainly no other sport does. Pit the Super Bowl against the World Series and what do you get? Youth versus age. The twenty-first century rocketing past the twentieth. One thing rising, another falling. A single Super Bowl halftime "wardrobe malfunction" has permeated public consciousness more fully than anything that's happened at the World Series since Bill Mazeroski shocked the Yankees and the nation in 1960. (What's that? You don't know anything about Mazeroski's homerun that . . . ? *Ahem.*)

No, the phenomenon of professional football—with its relentless specialization, its inordinately complex "strategic planning," its rapid assimilation of new technologies (can anyone imagine Namath with a radio in his helmet? Can anyone picture Jim Thorpe *in* a helmet?), its rhythm of quick bursts and pregnant pauses, its gleaming sensuality of (safe!) violence and sex, its worship of the youthful body, its intense drive for the jolting climax—spits our way of life back at us in neat three hour packages, Sunday after Sunday. We watch football and we see our world far more roundly than we ever see it on CNN. Many of us *feel* it as fully as we feel it anywhere. The NFL is us. No wonder we don face paint.

To the extent that there is a surging cult of pro football in our day it is at least partially bound up in an elaborate form of self-worship—which, of course, the NFL feeds on. Every cult—every culture—needs its symbols, its priests, its holy places, its icons, its laws, and its gods, and the NFL attentively furnishes them all. To my left, as I write, lies atop a filing cabinet my Super Bowl XL "locker room hat," with the word "Champions" emblazoned between the Steelers logo and the NFL logo. Is it by accident that the latter is positioned above the former? I doubt it. The placement is itself a subtle assertion of rule, authority, and might.

Former NFL player and cultural historian Michael Oriard vividly charts the league's cult-like ascendance in his illuminating book *Brand NFL: Making and Selling America's Favorite Sport.* Joe Namath, it turns out, was "the best thing to happen to the NFL since television"—not due to his effect on the league's role as custodian of the sport but rather on its development into a "multimedia entertainment business." Just as the NFL was searching for ways to enlarge its place in American life, Namath's celebrity in the late 1960s wed pro football to the emerging empire of hip in utterly memorable, if not always salubrious ways. Not only *Sports Illustrated* but *Time, Life, Esquire,* and *Playboy* felt compelled to regularly comment on the meaning of Namath, the person of Namath, the sheer fact of Namath. For his part, Namath, writes Oriard, became "the first athlete in any sport to be himself an advertisement for a lifestyle." Who can forget—try as we might—Namath hocking pantyhose?

That persona led thousands, of course, right back to the game—the NFL's game. For Christmas in 1974 my brother and I received presents we greeted with mighty portions of yuletide glee: official Joe Namath helmets, shoulder pads, and jerseys! The long arm of the NFL, via its nascent NFL Properties division, was reaching into our hearts and imaginations, connecting boys to a league in transforming ways, spawning identities rooted in whatever vision of life suited its own vision for its future.

Here's what I wonder: what kind of organization is it that provides us with everything we want, from extraordinary spectacles to godlike athletes to dancing girls? And what kind of people is it that accepts such offerings?

These are dangerous questions, costly to ask. And so we don't. (Only six weeks till training camp!)

But ask them we must—if that troubling first-century category "the world" and the older notion of "idolatry" are to have any contemporary meaning. What do these ancient words get at if not a people's steady refusal of the true pathway to life, and their accompanying preference for the counterfeit?

We, of course, stray toward worldliness and idolatry like children veer toward a candy shop. Lured by longing, excited by taste, we'll check out any peep show that comes along (from gossip pages to *Penthouse* pics), and try anything that whispers our name (from new hair colors to new wives). "An altered state of being / it's what everybody's looking for," croons singer-songwriter John Hiatt, and he's dead on. "Those who cling to worthless idols / forfeit the grace that could be theirs," warned a much earlier poet, the prophet Jonah, and he too nailed our miserable condition, as we, in a cockeyed quest for life, turn toward decay. Truly we are, of all creatures, most wretched.

Here's the thing, though, about idolatry, and what makes it particularly dangerous in our time: it is big business. It always has been, of course, an ever-reliable means of profit at the expense of the human soul. But in a time when unprecedented concentrations of human intelligence are dedicated to preying on our frailty with an ingenuity and cunning that must surely drive the Pentagon to envy, we've become playthings of the profiteers. The record on this is clear: we are no match for their wiles. All too easily, often blindly, we let them have their way.

So we must ask of the NFL what we must ask of any entity with the ability to touch our souls and shape our lives: does it have our best—our children's best—interests at heart? Is there good evidence it even *knows* our best interests? More particularly, to what lengths will it go to create a wholly faithful, devoted congregation—err, "fan base"?

And we must ask ourselves: should I be a part of it? Is it keeping me on the true way? Or luring me away?

Despite these critical cautions, idolatry and worldliness are not the whole story, not by a long shot. Evil exists only by corrupting that which is good, and in football there remains considerable good to be savored and preserved. Football, to put it differently, may lead not to the forfeiture of grace but to a richer experience of it. And like most experiences of grace, it involves people and takes root in a place. For me, that place is Pittsburgh.

Having lived here for eight years now, I sense more fully the region's rhythms, the slow shifting of seasons and sports, each sport with its season, each season incomplete without its sports. The traditions surrounding high school football run especially deep, I've learned. In our introductory history class I require students to write research papers and urge them to use local sources. It's the world of football that many of the local kids turn to, rooting out the legends and stories, investigating and retelling tales of yore. The most memorable papers are the ones that have to do with the students' own participation in rituals and rivalries that go back decades, often to the early twentieth century.

These young researchers are, I think, laying hold of a way to keep faith with the world of their childhood, a world that was, at its best, a place of grace, with football near to the heart of it. College, they uneasily sense, offers not a way to settle into what they know but a course that will shake them from it. The authors they read, the people they meet, the training they acquire: much of it prepares them for departure from their home—especially likely given the area's declining economic fortunes in these post-industrial, post-local United States. In this uncertain climate, high school football feels like the ground itself. So they dig in.

It's this that is so striking about football season here, and no doubt elsewhere: the impulse to look to football as a pathway to that which matters. Football in western Pennsylvania consistently gives rise to an experience, however ephemeral and elusive, of roots, of renewal, of home—a long hoped-for reunion not just with friends and kin, but with life itself. Why is this?

There are regional realities at play, to be sure, along with the more common experiences of loyal fans anywhere. *New York Times* writer Jere Longman describes Pittsburgh as an "appealing but frayed city of immigrants" for good reason. It's an area frayed not just by sharp declines in jobs and population—a loss between 1970 and 1990 of 158,000 manufacturing jobs and 289,000 residents—but also by the immigrant experience itself, as the traces of ethnic particularity, so unexpectedly soluble, soften, and what's left is blended into America's dull mainstream sheen, youthful faces that register "cool" and "fun" and "work" but little more. The longing for that something more, though—and for something lost—builds and deepens, and ends up whooshing into the already huge, ever-enlarging world of football.

In the midst of the Steelers' 2005 surge to the Super Bowl, one Pittsburgh expatriate, Hollywood writer and director David Hollander, described in the *Post-Gazette* his own Steelers-sparked moment of longing and renewal following a decisive season-saving victory against the Bears. After Steelers running back Jerome Bettis had at a crucial point in the game knocked Bears über-linebacker Brian Urlacher to the ground and charged into the end zone, Hollander writes, "my boy looked at me with alarm and asked why Daddy had tears running down his face." To his knowing readers—his true countrymen, as it were—he confesses, "It's hard to explain to a kid being raised in Southern California the meaning of loving a team as much as any kid from Pittsburgh loves the Steelers." His shot at an explanation strikes chords—grace chords: "We love our Steelers because, at their best, our Steelers love the game. We love our Steelers because they play with power and joy and clarity, through pain and age and sore knees . . ." In a rapidly fraying world, the Steelers, remarkably, "have remained the Steelers."

This is why Vic Ketchman, formerly of Pittsburgh, now the senior editor of the Jacksonville Jaguars team website, describes the Steelers as "the team for all the ones who like the old things," people who "don't want fast food, who don't want to live in a new bedroom community and pay association fees, who don't want progress forced upon us. Pittsburgh is an old place," he concludes. And the Steelers? They're "like coming home."

It does amount to something of a paradox, this notion that anything connected to today's NFL could possibly stand against what Ketchman bitterly and euphemistically calls "progress." But judging by the history of Pittsburgh, football can indeed be an agent that binds us to a place, to family and friends, perhaps even to a noble ethic. These effects seem to me all the evidence one requires to conclude that grace, of a certain kind, has been here. *Is* here.

It doesn't happen everywhere, and doesn't automatically continue where it does happen. The people of Pittsburgh are fortunate to have had on their side a powerful local family, the Rooneys, who have owned and operated the team since patriarch Art Rooney bought the team for $2,500 in 1933. Holding doggedly to their ideals for sport and community amidst the torrent of the past half-century, the Rooneys have sought, often with painful compromises, to foster a team that even in the financially driven maelstrom of professional sports is bound to its community, in body and spirit. Embodying fidelity, they have sought players and coaches who not only excel at the game but who also love Pittsburgh, "the tough, sweet city of workers," in poet Maggie Anderson's words.

These Pittsburghers love the team—and the Rooneys—right back. And in loving, they gain a taste of life—or, better, a rich sampling of a deeper, truer life. In a faith-starved world, in a land being slowly emptied of meaningful ritual and intimate human ties, they, like modern folk the world round, turn to sport as a means of participation in the friendship, the laughter, the play, and the joy that lie at the heart of any healthy and flourishing human world. In doing so they become responsible bearers of traditions that make such vital experiences possible.

But football, for all the good it may bring to a people and a place, is not the final good, whatever the pretensions of the NFL or its devotees. The spirit of truth must always check the spirit of the age. And truth be told, in this age our spirits settle for far too little. Football, cell phones, vacations, careers: these tantalize with the promise of plenty, yet leave us hungry for more.

To the starving, a piece of bread looks like a meal. The healthy know it's not; that if it isn't augmented by more nutritious fare the suffering will, in some form, go on. More, much more, is needed if health is to be achieved.

At its best, sport may lead us more fully into an experience of health, an experience of community, play, joy. But this happens only if it is enfolded within a grander, richer participation in life, in which another set of rites and symbols and songs takes us more deeply into gratitude and grace, sourced in the Creator and centered on the cross.

I describe, of course, the way of the church, the beautiful dance of God's own family, whose existence in this age is centered on the hope of welcoming into its way hungry people, distressed people—yet people who, for whatever else they may yet lack, have already come to know grace in rich, concrete, and satisfying ways. Those concerned to love these could do worse than join them in the stands come fall, cheering for all they're worth. Grace, after all, goes both ways, and touches down in highly improbable fashion—even, I'm guessing, through face paint and cutting boards.

—2007

The Republic of Baseball

THERE ARE THOSE, WRITES Charles Fountain, "who see baseball as succor to the soul, a spirit that binds eras and generations." To say the least.

In early twentieth-century Puerto Rico, "baseball was what fisherman thought about when they cast their lines and farmers when they harvested sugar cane," writes Larry Tye in his biography of Satchel Paige. Richard Peterson remembers true love in rough and dirty midtwentieth-century Pittsburgh. "My buddies and I played baseball every day, beginning in the cold, soggy spring, through the dog days of summer, until the chilly fall rains turned our fields of dreams into mud. With neighborhood rivalries and individual pride at stake, we played a punishing, reckless brand of baseball that often went beyond a love of the game itself. . . . I lived for those games and couldn't imagine what I would do with my life if I didn't play some day for the Pirates."

Peterson was in college and on his way to becoming an English professor by the time his Pirates defied history, logic, and bookies everywhere by defeating the Yankees in the 1960 World Series. As the season came to a close the town erupted into *fiesta* and melted into love, more than 100,000—a sixth of its population—showing up *at midnight* to welcome the team back after it seized the National League pennant. "Ever see anything like this?" asked a New York writer to the Pirates' Cleb Labine, who had played on the Dodgers' championship team five years before. "Not like this, dad. Even Brooklyn was never like this."

Even Brooklyn. The words still sing and sting, a half-century later. New York had been to baseball what New Orleans was to jazz, the epicenter of a great national passion, utterly defined by a proud and inspired devotion to it. In his 1994 *Baseball* documentary Ken Burns, himself Brooklyn born, beautifully captured the earthy intricacies of this allegiance, recording for posterity the language, syntax, and inflections of a trio of winsome and articulate New Yorkers—Steven Jay Gould, Billy Crystal, and Doris Kearns Goodwin—recalling the baseball of their childhoods. Their testimonials warmly reinforce Robert E. Murphy's contention that New York was then "so dense with baseball fans that it took three teams to represent it, each of them deeply rooted and closely identified with the place in which it played." Succor to the soul indeed.

But even among its New York rivals Brooklyn's attachment to its team stood out. Through most of the nineteenth century Brooklyn, incorporated as a separate city, had cultivated a careful distance from Manhattan. Against the countervailing wisdom of the age many wished it to remain that way. "One grew tall and became the center of most American things," writes Murphy in *After Many a Summer: The Passing of the Giants and Dodgers and a Golden Age in New York Baseball.* "The other grew wide and became the center of little except its own way of life and, for a while, even more than its mighty neighbor, of baseball." By the 1950s, "all the country knew that Brooklyn was the Dodgers and the Dodgers were Brooklyn," with Ebbets Field the blessed site of holy union. After decades of often bathetic failure, the team became a force following World War II, winning the 1955 World Series and numerous pennants. "Never had Brooklyn, intimate with baseball for more than 100 years, held a team so close to its heart," Murphy, himself a small child in the 1950s, remarks.

But Murphy's book is decidedly not memoir. It is history, and history at its best: impelled by a love that sharpens intelligence and deepens vision. His book, in fact, is hardly about the game of baseball at all—it's rather about the Dodgers and Giants, New York City, and the (losing) battle to keep them together. With piercing judgment and tart irony he renders the injustice, injury, and pain the loss of these teams inflicted not only on New York, but on the nation itself.

Murphy's committed style may draw arguments, but his efforts to be scrupulously fair cannot be denied. His ample knowledge of the evidence and the historiography helps him present a richly complex story, with no simple, single villainous presence. Horace Stoneham and Walter O'Malley, owners of the Giants and Dodgers respectively, were facing considerable economic, social, and civic pressures that left them uncertain about their abilities to keep the teams financially sound in the disorienting mid-century world. Local identities were rapidly thinning, stretched by new forms of locomotion and weakened by dreams that promised truer identities elsewhere. Baseball, "inner-city-based, incompatible with the automobile, was looking old," Murphy notes, with all major league teams struggling at the gate as the decade, year by year, revealed its goods—among them commercial jet service from the East Coast to the West, just beginning in 1958 (the year, not coincidentally, the Dodgers and Giants left town). There was certainly wonder in that. America was not just "moving again." It was moving in all kinds of ways it had never moved before. Would it take baseball with it? The answer didn't seem at all certain.

Along with granting a widespread perplexity, Murphy even finds evidence of good faith on the part of both the teams' owners and the city officials who fought to keep them in New York. What he doesn't find is *enough* good faith, at least not enough to justify the decisions of the owners to take the teams and run. Both teams were making money, the Dodgers loads of it—a model franchise, it seemed, the envy of the league. New York's civic leaders scrambled, often dysfunctionally, to find ways to meet O'Malley's insistent demands for a new stadium, one that could lure people beyond the borough back into town. It was not enough.

For his part, O'Malley, who had gained control of the Dodgers by 1950, claimed a profound commitment to Brooklyn. Others aren't so sure, Murphy among them. "Whether or not he actually loved Brooklyn," Murphy concludes, "he didn't care as much about improving the borough as he did about having his own ballpark, built and located to his own specifications." O'Malley's new stadium in LA would be his lasting treasure. All the treasure left in Brooklyn was memory. In his famous "obituary" of the Brooklyn Dodgers, Dick Young of the *New York Daily News* pronounced judgment with mordant disdain. "The cause of death was acute greed, followed by severe political complications." The Dodgers had died "the healthiest corpse in sports history."

But in those bewildering Cold War days, with the nation poised, as Robert Wuthnow puts it, between promise and peril, did all of this contention about baseball, all of this upset, truly matter?

It wasn't just the ordinary fans who felt deeply that it did. Perhaps the single most illuminating facet of Murphy's book is his recapturing of the language and arguments New York's leaders used as they faced what was, to them, a truly momentous situation, charged with civic import. Brooklyn congressman Emmanuel Celler forcefully contended that team owners should not see themselves as businessmen but rather as "sportsmen who were satisfied just to make a living while serving the interests of their fans." New York City Council President (and Brooklynite) Abe Stark, in a statement before Congress, stated his view just as sharply. "It is my belief," he declared, "that a baseball franchise morally belongs to the people of a community. It is not the personal property of any individual, to be removed at the slightest whim." George V. McLaughlin—one-time New York City police commissioner, part-owner of the Dodgers, president of the Brooklyn Trust Company, and friend of O'Malley—spoke in the same way as he led a last-ditch effort to purchase the Giants from Stoneham. His not-for-profit group, he explained in a letter to Stoneham, was comprised of *"public-spirited citizens."*

Read Benjamin Franklin's autobiography and you'll find this very phrase, and phrases like it, used repeatedly. It's the old republican tongue, insisting with a conviction born of bitter experience that purely private interests were finally corrupting of the ends that humans might— must—achieve, including, above all, a significant sense of solidarity and commonwealth, a prosperity born of mutuality. Citizen Franklin started a fire company, published a newspaper, and launched a debating club. Among McLaughlin's concerns was baseball. Both men knew that such distinct yet interconnected activity was wonderfully and mysteriously necessary for the prospering of the whole. More ominously, they sensed that if these institutions, and a hundred like them, were absent, a dark expansive vacuum would emerge, to be inevitably filled by forces boasting an authority born of might, that could only degrade a citizenry into a warping dependency.

"Why was not one owner willing to stand up and say 'no' to the abandonment of New York fans?" wonders Murphy, wandering around in that void decades later. Why indeed? "It was now clear where baseball owners stood: for themselves and economic opportunity, rather than for devoted fans and a game's traditions."

This was the disturbing reality the departure of the Dodgers and Giants made clear. In its aftermath, some began to fight, in the words of Senator Estes Kefauver—another concerned citizen—to "return baseball to the American people." None fought harder than Branch Rickey; probably none cared more. Rickey, the most historically significant baseball man of the century, was the executive with the brightest mind and sharpest vision for all facets of the game, including its social context. Born in 1881, Rickey had been part-owner of the Dodgers in the 1940s while also directing its day-to-day operations (including the operation to integrate black players into the majors)—until O'Malley, who detested him, forced him out. In an appearance before Congress in the spring of 1960, Rickey starkly opined that "the major league owners need to be saved from themselves." He himself was in the midst of just such a salvation effort, the attempt to launch a new major league, the "Continental League," which would, among other things, feature the kind of revenue-sharing among its eight teams that would later make rich the National Football League but also admirably competitive, keeping even small-market franchises in the game. Baseball owners resoundingly resisted (and still do).

In his sprightly history of this effort, *Bottom of the Ninth*, Michael Shapiro notes that Rickey "threw himself into the job with the energy of a young man who saw a higher purpose in his work." Baseball, Rickey believed, was, simply, good for the nation. Beyond that it was simply *good*, and should thus be preserved. But he also knew that such preservation was necessarily a civic act—hence his willingness to battle the owners in Congress for the possibility of restoring and renewing the game. As Shapiro puts it, for Rickey "the game was a noble enterprise that the Senate was in a position to deliver to an eager nation."

The Continental League failed, never playing a game. The owners cagily co-opted Rickey's plan, deciding to permit franchise expansion for the first time in fifty-some years rather than grant the new circuit major league status. By this time professional baseball was under threat for the first time by another sport, the far more disciplined, hierarchical, and entertainment-savvy National Football League. Many predicted baseball's demise. But eventually it found ways to latch on to the postwar economic juggernaut and ride into the expansive consumerist future, regaining some of its popularity in the 1970s by belatedly embracing free agency, and riffing along with the neo-traditionalist turn the nation took through the 80s and 90s, in the aftermath of Watergate and Vietnam.

It's a story in many ways of ascent—costly ascent, as Charles Fountain's *Under the March Sun: The Story of Spring Training* makes clear. In probing the underlying workings of the political economy that sustains the major leagues, he provides striking evidence of what the economist Joseph Schumpeter was getting at when at mid-century he described capitalism as a system propelled by "creative destruction." The alliance of private capital, civic energy, and middle-class affluence has certainly been creative: spring training has gone from a spare, money-losing necessity to a revenue-raising, profile-enhancing piece of promotion for town and team alike. Cities and counties throughout Florida and Arizona now vie for teams like drones in quest of the queen bee, and the golden honey of capital has flowed.

Fountain's account of the wooing of the Astros to Osceola Country, Florida, in the mid-1980s, at the moment competition between towns for suitors was being jacked up to a new level, is nicely illustrative. "So what do you want? asked the county. The Astros began tentatively, afraid of asking for too much. Well, how about four practice fields, they said. Done, said the county. What else?" By winter of 1985 Astros general manager Al Rosen was one satisfied man. "I don't think there is another spring training facility comparable to ours," he announced.

That judgment didn't hold up for even a decade; the facility, Fountain writes, became "quickly obsolete." Other teams and towns had seized on Osceola's example and pushed for more plush, sophisticated accommodations. Some efforts, like the misguided development of "Baseball City" in Polk County, Florida, to which the Kansas City Royals had committed, flopped, and for good reason. "Had Baseball City been real," judges Fountain, "had it been supported by a local population and a local government and a business community, spring training and the Royals might have had a chance." But this "city" was, in the end, merely a brand, as vacuous as the names that now bedeck our stadiums. "Calling it 'Baseball City' . . . couldn't make it a community," Fountain concludes, and suggests that in this high-stakes game success requires "a high degree of coordination and cooperation among the state, the host cities, and the various civic groups"—not just "civic involvement," but "*citizen* involvement."

One can almost see Franklin, and a little while later, Alexis de Tocqueville, smiling. Almost. It would be comforting to imagine that even capital, in the end, must submit to what Fountain calls the "real," this solidity born of human devotion, affection, and persisting ties. But that's not quite the way it works. Just ask Brooklyn.

Yet our abiding, sentimental faith that market-driven enterprise can safeguard and nurture our most necessary ideals, practices, and institutions persists. Haven't we endured enough history to know better? If neither education nor government nor church nor the family nor health nor the sky nor even finance itself is safe in the market's hands—despite the vigilance of good men and women striving to make the system work for us, not merely for itself—why should we give baseball over to it?

All fans know that three words, whether spoken by villains or saints, kill the spirit of whatever sport of which they're said: *It's a business.* Baseball is not a business, any more than is marriage, or teaching first grade, or playing four-square. If we want to raise boys and girls who will come, like the aging Satchel Paige, to preach "the sanctity of the double steal and the blessedness of the bunt," we will find ways to preserve and protect this treasure. And chances are, if our children learn to feel the sanctity of the double steal, they'll come to know other realms of sanctity too—and perhaps gain the courage to construct ways of guarding them.

—2009

Play On!

I DIDN'T WANT TO move to Brazil. The reasons were many, and readily discernable to anyone with a whit of insight. But the one that played most painfully upon my day-to-day longings had something to do with this: the Pirates had won the World Series the previous fall. The Steelers had won the Super Bowl four out of the previous six Januarys. A native of western Pennsylvania, thirteen years old, I loved sports. And I knew victory. Both were sweet. Indescribably sweet.

I could not have known that within two years I would be swept up in a sports storm that even now bursts from my memory with force. Upon hitting Brazilian soil in the summer of 1980 I began what turned out to be a shockingly rapid conversion to *futebol*, trading glove and cap for *kichute* and *camisa*, the soccer cleats and team shirts my new friends wore. Most were *Americanos*, yes, but where it mattered they were Brazilian: on the field. They took me and my brothers into the wonder-world of Brazilian soccer—*futebol arte*, as the Brazilians joyed to call it—where legends lived and heroes danced, sweeping across the field with vibrancy and focus and delight, magicians with a ball, making magic for the world.

And the world was watching. This I discovered early on, as the national team—known simply as the *Seleção* ("selection")—played its way into the 1982 World Cup, the storm that would take my past experiences of sporting enthusiasm to new degrees of intensity. As the Cup neared, the sense grew, game by game, that this Brazilian team was unusual, even by Brazil's Olympian standards, armed with a midfield quartet as creative and dominant as any since the fabled days of soccer's undisputed greatest player ever, Brazil's Pelé, who had led the country to World Cup championships in 1958, 1962, and 1970. I was scrambling to learn Portuguese by reading, dictionary in hand, the weekly sports magazine *Placar*, trying to absorb the scene as fully as possible. By the time the world's soccer powers converged upon Spain that June anticipation had turned to climax, a month-long climax, filled with mystery, stars, jubilation—and defeat.

But first came the victories. Brazil, led by fabulous athletes with mythical names—Zico, Socrates, Falcão, Leandro—dispatched of its early opponents with such potent *joie de vivre* that the final victory seemed only a blink away. Russia, Scotland, and New Zealand fell in the first round, mere apprentices. All Brazil swelled with glee. Argentina and Italy awaited in the second round, past champions both, always dangerous. But the Brazil-Argentina showdown proved to be simply one more Brazilian show. Now a victory over Italy would mean a semi-final berth.

To that point Italy had played drab, uninspired soccer. Suddenly it found inspiration. Brazil went for broke, putting its *jogo bonito* ("beautiful game") on brilliant display, with an unending medley of fluid passes and pounding shots. But in what turned out to be the greatest game of the tournament, Italy held them to two goals and managed three of their own, taking advantage of the ever-attacking Brazilian midfield and a surprisingly weak goaltender. The all but certain coronation never came. Italy went on to win its third *Copa*, creating legends of its own.

The anguish of the loss was exquisite, the precise opposite of the overwhelming, samba-fired joy that had rumbled and raged through the country the previous two weeks. All Brazil—*all Brazil*—had shut down for its five games: no shoppers served, no mail delivered, no gas pumped. The *festa* smacked of eternity; the joy at victory called up weddings and homecomings. They greeted the defeat with abject disbelief, a mourning echoing deeply down the soul of a long-floundering, ever-rising nation. The dream abruptly died—for a time, at least. But although Brazil has since won the *Copa* twice, its victorious sides have never equaled the grace and verve of that '82 *Seleção*. Even in defeat, it made history.

It was the public nature of the joy that so affected me. Just before moving to Brazil I had had a taste of it, when I'd watched the (indeed miraculous) American hockey team skate to the gold in the 1980 Olympics, Cold War passion and sporting love coursing through the nation's heart, and my own. When the United States defeated the Soviets, I had marveled—and, instinctively, rejoiced—at seeing the news clips that showed cars pulled off along the roadside and people spontaneously breaking into "God Bless America." This was my point of reference for national celebration and patriotic unity. But what had happened in Brazil during those two weeks completely eclipsed it.

I was changed forever. When I entered Brazil in July of 1980 I was wearing the brassy yellow t-shirt an uncle had given me at a farewell party. It featured a muscular eagle wrapped in stars and stripes, with a banner waving beneath it that read "American and Proud of It." When I re-entered the United States four years later, I was sporting yellow again. But this time it was the shimmering, golden, green-trimmed jersey of the *Seleção*. I was all-American no more.

It's striking that this is the title we drape across the shoulders of our athletic champions: *All-American*. The 1940 film *Knute Rockne, All-American* suggests, with blunt but sweet directness, how this came to be. "The life of Knute Rockne," ran a prefatory declamation as the film began, "is its own dedication to the Youth of America and to the finest ideals of courage, character, and sportsmanship for all the world. Knute Rockne was a great and vital force in molding the spirit of modern America . . ."

America, an invented and enlightened nation, always required this molding, this worried attention to spirit and shape. But by the turn of the twentieth century something new had to be found to ensure that the recently electrified, urbanized, imperial nation had a great and upstanding citizenry to match—especially in view of the kaleidoscopic movement of migrants and immigrants that was transfiguring cities from Boston to LA. Modern industry had made modern cities. But it was still human beings—energetic, anarchic—who would inhabit them. Once outside the factories, what would people do? This was the troubling question.

Sport became the city's way of preserving the ancient field, and sports teams a means of preserving the venerable village, both so necessary for any vital experience of the good life. As the maelstrom of modern living wove people into a colossal tangle, open space and communal impulses took new forms, and anxious gatekeepers were left hoping that, despite the ruckus of it all, something like a dance might emerge.

Sport—closely tied to religion—was one of the dances they turned to, and with an intensity that can only be called innocent.

Knute Rockne, All-American gives a taste of this innocence. The child of parents who immigrated from Norway in 1895, young Knute, jammed with thousands of other children into Jane Addams' Chicago, eventually finds his way onto a football field, and soon after declares to his parents that "We're all Americans now—especially me: I'm a left end!" Years later, after he had become head coach at the University of Notre Dame, Rockne wins his players' allegiance with a passionate, gruff, principled approach to coaching, and to life. The film is now remembered as a Ronald Reagan movie, and Reagan's George Gipp delivers the tribute to Rockne that reveals precisely what the accolade "All-American" was to encompass. "He's given us something they don't teach in schools," Gipp tells Mrs. Rockne. "Something clean and strong inside—not just coaching but a way of living, something we'll never forget."

It's a jock flick best seen as a dream, a species of all-American romance. Like all romances, but especially those of this variety, it seeks to preserve cherished ideals: virtue, harmony, joy, fraternity. But this act of preservation comes, it turns out, at the expense of the persons depicted. We can't believe in these characters; such nobility and fellow-feeling and all-around jollity go down way too easily. We know there must be another side of the American story, however dreary and dark.

In her book *The Real All Americans: The Team That Changed a Game, a People, and a Nation*, Sally Jenkins gives it to us, revealing, among other things, the mangled, unholy relationship between modern sport and modern America that *Knute Rockne* would not probe. And she shows us why we, in our times, must be on guard even against sport.

Jenkins's tale centers on the remarkable and forgotten connection between the game of football and that part of American history that *Rockne*, Reagan, and any number of other all-Americans have so easily elided: the fate of the indigenous people who fell before the mighty all-American engine. Her candor intensifies pathos. If she too tilts steeply toward romance (of a distinctively postmodern variety: not the romance of the conqueror, but of the conquered), she writes with subtlety and evenhandedness, with a pleasing sympathy to all sides of this ugly, beautiful story.

In the midst of the great modern charge, Jenkins shows, the feverishly popular game of football indeed helped us define ourselves as a nation—but not necessarily in ways we can be proud of. "The game, like the country in which it was invented, was a rough, bastardized thing that jumped up out of the mud," she notes. By the late nineteenth century the annual Yale-Princeton matchup was so huge that churches in Manhattan held services an hour early to ensure that fans could make it to the game; 40,000 showed up at Polo Grounds in 1890 to watch the Ivies slug it out. The era of the mass spectacle was underway, though even football, remarkably, was an arena that reflected the persisting grip of old-stock elites on the nation's public life: it was Harvard, Yale, and Princeton that were the titans of the gridiron.

This is where the lowly Carlisle Indians come into the story, and where the marriage of nation and sport is revealed in all its corrupt complexity—as well as its redemptive worth.

Carlisle was a team of actual Indians, students at an experimental school just outside of Harrisburg, Pennsylvania, founded in the fall of 1879 when its earnest, quintessentially inner-directed architect, Captain Richard Henry Pratt, corralled a pan-Indian collection of youngsters (including many who were the children of chiefs), back East for (re) education. His sympathy for and devotion to the Indians are just as evident as his own repellant cultural stamp; among his mottoes was "Kill the Indian, save the man." It's no wonder Jenkins describes the school as a "violent social experiment," where English was required, braided hair (on boys) was shorn, and members of tribes were separated.

And yet Pratt loved the Indians, Jenkins makes clear. When several years after its launch some boys asked permission to start a football team, he, nervous about the violence of the game, cautiously said yes, and then watched in wonder. "Their grace and exceptional speed in getting all over the field was a revelation," he recalled. In 1900 Harvard's coach (as it turns out, the grandson of Ralph Waldo Emerson) declared that football was "the ultimate expression of Anglo-Saxon superiority"—precisely the kind of culture-defining conceit that irked Pratt. When he gave the go to football, he did so with two utterly characteristic conditions: first, that the players practice charity and self-control in the face of provocation; second, that they prepare themselves to shortly "whip the biggest football team in the country."

They fulfilled both conditions amply, and managed to change history too, creating in effect the game we know today. In the face of the steam-rolling, bone-crunching Anglo-Saxon style, the Indians, with the same poise, mystery, and wit that gave Colonel Custer and friends fits, showed the now-watching world another way to play. "They had invented a whole new brand of game," Jenkins writes. "Carlisle football, mixing the run, pass, and kick with elements of surprise, was the game of the future. The traditional powers would cling to their old tactics at their peril." Between 1911 and 1913, taking on the most dominant, best-financed teams in the country, the team would pile up thirty-eight victories against only three defeats. After the climactic episode in the book, the 1912 Jim Thorpe-led defeat of the powerhouse Army Cadets, the *New York Times* itself declared Carlisle's "the most perfect brand of football ever seen in America."

Their innovating coach, Glenn Scobey "Pop'" Warner, had helped channel the genius of the Indians' own place, people, and time into a form that has stood the test of time (including, contra the blatantly false claim of *Knute Rockne*, the perfecting of the forward pass as a primary offensive weapon). And it was Warner who lauded their achievement most poignantly. "Whenever I see one of those All American teams," he mused in his memoirs, "I cannot help but think what an eleven could have been selected from those *real* All Americans who blazed such a trail of glory."

Can the trail of glory ever truly emerge from anything so tangled in the thorns of this corrupt plane? For as readily as *Knute Rockne* applies varnish, Jenkins strips it. She forces us to confront the malign motives, the violent impulses, the idolatrous yearnings—often on a grand, national scale—that modern sport has been mixed up in since its birth.

This seedy reality is bound to trouble those charged with setting themselves apart as a holy nation, those Christ himself described as "not of the world any more than I am of the world." Sports, like so many other social forms concocted in the modern world—from the shopping mall to the stock market to the U.S. Congress to the U.N.—seems coated in compromise, lethal to body and soul. These social forms attract a degrading kind of allegiance, effected by both brazen seduction and sickly dependence, and leave decent folk longing for far truer forms of membership, of belonging, of citizenship.

And yet, as all of these stories make evident, it's both wheat and tares that fill our fields, tares that invariably choke life, wheat that miraculously gives it. There is no escaping this tangle. There is only the persisting need to dedicate ourselves to preserving the good that is miraculously here, and by that preserving expose the evil that threatens it. If sports in our day have become the playthings of catastrophically irresponsible corporations, and if becoming a fan so often turns into a hollow, pseudo-religious semblance of true belonging, there yet remains the undeniable beauty of the sports themselves to uphold, and the marvelous reality of the actual human beings, the creatures of God almighty, who find themselves so irresistibly drawn to them.

Consider the story Jenkins tells about the Carlisle-Yale game of 1896, in the early years of Carlisle's football history. The Indians were coming off of a brutal 22–6 loss to Princeton, after which the *Philadelphia Press* had chortled, "The race with a civilization and a history won the day. It was a clear victory of mind over physical force." Just a few days later Carlisle was to take its grandest stage yet, Polo Grounds, to play mighty Yale. The team was a curiosity in a nation of citified consumers, and the game attracted a huge crowd, including Russell Sage, the railway magnate, philanthropist, and sometime politician, who played host to Pratt for the occasion. After Carlisle went up by a score early on, Yale came back and took a 12–6 lead into the closing minutes. But near the game's end the Carlisle left end broke away from a pileup with a mighty burst of strength and spurted down the field for a touchdown. The unthinkable was happening.

And then it happened again—this time in the other direction. As Carlisle was lining up to kick the extra point, a late whistle sounded. One of the referees—a Yale alum and also (in a situation not uncharacteristic of the day) the Carlisle coach—was calling the play back. The players were stunned. The crowd started to boo, louder and louder. The Indians threatened to leave, talked out of it only by Pratt himself.

The clock wound down, and the game ended. But as it did the crowd, breaking into a mighty ovation, took a completely unexpected step—one giant step for mankind, as it were: it stormed the field and carried the Indians off the field. The *New York Sun*, as did most of the press, hoisted the players as well, declaring, with sudden historical clarity, that the now infamous call was "characteristic . . . of nearly all the crimes committed against the Indians by the whites, for it was accomplished by the man of all men who should have looked out for their interests and their rights." After the game Mrs. Sage herself took off her corsage and pinned it on Carlisle quarterback Frank Cayou, who had scored the first touchdown.

How we glory in exceptional play, we creatures of God. We delight in honest, fierce competition. We thrill to witness the fruit of difficult, demanding training. We watch, enchanted, as our athletes hurtle themselves toward their dreams, whole-hearted, focused on the prize, acting together, giving all. We sense our spirits rise. It's just a game, we know, we know. But it hints, somehow, at that which lies beneath the game, yet is also deeply integral to life on this wondrous earth. The swell of admiration, the giving of affection, the ennobling of sacrifice: it all reminds us so sweetly of who we finally are, and where we're bound.

We're certainly bound for a land that transcends these particular identities—American, Brazilian, Norse, Lakota—even as it redeems and honors them. And it's this difficult but wonderful tension, the tension between the universal and the particular, that is perhaps the most redemptive effect of modern sport. It previews a day when we will know ourselves for what we at root are: human beings, distinct but united, many but one, destined for an eternal dance—destined for play—in the kingdom of God.

Until that day, those who know that hope can surely honor it with beautiful dives, bravura goals, bountiful cheers. Somewhere, some confused teenager—or marginal man, or aged woman—will see.

And will know.

—2008

FAITH

The Lure of the Flesh,
The Evasion of Flesh and Blood

Discovering the Way of Virtue

WHAT TO DO ABOUT this corruption? That's the question I keep asking myself.

Daily the misshapen take their places before us. No pretty sight, this. A mother beds her children's babysitter, who proceeds to kill the father of her children. A man guns down his ex-wife at the burial site of their daughter. Parents place photographs of their own children on pornographic websites. Of course, one needn't read the newspaper to learn of such Cain-and-Abel stories. There are more subtle varieties.

Corruption: what was whole, now bizarrely deformed. Identity lost, but not quite gone. Our circumstance could not be more obvious: we live in a diminished state. We are corruptible. We are self-corrupting. We find this tolerable, most days.

If we are corrupt, from what shape have we departed? Has anyone a vision of our pre-entropic condition? Has anyone an understanding of who or what we were to be? Hints abound, provided we can get past the subterfuge and draw near to the voices that bear witness to our intended form.

I recently asked my grandmother, a widow now ten years, about my grandfather's boyhood. As a child he had bounced around West Virginia's eastern panhandle and had the accent to prove it: the memory of him singing "Victory in Jesus" in his full-throated, straight-from-the-hills baritone still haunts and inspires me.

That day my grandmother let me in on a part of the story I'd never heard. Pap's father, it turns out, was killed when the boy was only three months old. While he was trying to break up a barroom fight someone smashed him over the head with a concrete block. My grandfather's mother farmed him out to various relatives over the years. It's no wonder he married before he was twenty.

After learning this I was struck by a curious thought: my grandfather never stopped being the son of a father he never knew. No barroom tragedy could alter that. No such reversal is possible. Once a son, always a son.

Could it be that who we are, at the most elemental level, is sons and daughters? Scratch a "human," find somebody's little girl or boy? And might it follow, then, that if I am to gain a deep-seated sense of my true form, I must begin to act the part? I must learn to fill the shape of a son, a daughter, *the departure from which defines my corruption?*

Our kinship titles are, after all, freighted with moral obligation, and obligation emerges always from underlying moral structures sourced in God himself. If I, the father of three, am urged to *be* a father, I know what I must do: take responsibility for my very flesh and blood, be affectionately present in their lives, become a source of strength and correction. To not do this is to fail to *be* a father. In the same way, one who behaves in a "sisterly" or "brotherly" manner moves easily alongside the other, boosting and rebuking, imparting care. "The Brotherhood of Man" was nothing if not a moral imperative.

The power of these terms, even across different cultures, to obligate us to an ethic of caretaking bears witness to our true natures, our true identities: we are born into a web of kinship relations, an immediate community, that we are responsible to maintain. These relationships are not optional; they are inalienable; and they tell us who we should be. When I fail as a husband or brother, I fail, in the end, to be who I am. This is sin, a sign of my corrupted condition. My own life is littered with such signs.

Several years ago my youngest brother was going through a turbulent time during his college years. In the midst of his difficulties my sister and her husband had their first child. I recall my father mentioning my brother's situation one day and remarking, with no small amount of conviction, "He needs to stay around here, he needs to be an uncle. He's an uncle now."

Here's my brother, I thought, neck-deep in a crisis, and Dad wants him to *be an uncle?!* How odd! How quaint and old-fashioned. He's in college(!), after all—he can't just drop out. He could use some good counseling, some time away, perhaps, surrounded by learned and caring people. But *be an uncle??* That sort of mountain-talk had no resonance with me.

Then I became a father. And after a few years it became pretty hard to ignore the reality that I wasn't much of one. I slowly began to sense that this ugly failure was causally connected to the awful, eerie void I had been trying to fill with intellectual pursuits, aesthetic delights, or just a few occasional extra hours of sleep. Worst of all, I began to sense that my failures as a father were undeniably connected to my shortcomings as a husband, as a brother, as a son. I had the titles, but I did not own them. My dad, to my (classic) surprise, had uttered a great truth: what I needed most of all—I could deny it no more—was to learn to be what I already was.

My own quest for "identity," for the "real me," had led down a barren path. You can't fail to fill your intended shape and not experience the effects of elemental dissolution. A father who is not a father cannot be much else for long; even what he has will be taken from him. This is a state Scripture calls "cursed."

Our malign tendencies are two, and we vacillate between them. At the one pole, we distance ourselves from our flesh and blood, our kin, misconstruing them as obstacles that prohibit us from "being ourselves." Or, running the other way, we meld ourselves into our kin, tightly tying our porous sense of identity to them in an inordinate fashion. We tend either to starve our own of the love we owe them, or we suffocate them with something we may call love but is in fact an attempt to enliven our own barren souls by means of an unholy synergy. Either way, we evade our responsibility to help mold our kin into the men and women they must become, dooming future generations to reenact our own shortcomings.

Surely this is the most damning evidence of our race's corruption: whole cities of fathers who refuse to give themselves over to their own offspring, numberless mothers who touch the fruit of their wombs mainly to take, neither parent willing or able to move their little ones along toward their intended shapes. Our tendency is to follow the dictates of what New Testament authors call our "flesh" and evade our very flesh and blood. We were born to be caregivers, but we are careless. We shrink from the ideal form that will ultimately judge us. And then we worship our deformity, or else ignore it.

This is not the sort of reading of the human condition one usually gets from the prominent storytellers of our age. Modern eyes see darkness in different places. You are an "individual," the great modern mythmakers tell us. You are a "self," and your duty is to it alone. Leave the medieval cave of family, church, tradition. Discover the sunshine of autonomy, and allow its rays to nurture you to health.

Consider the well-worn trope of the "identity crisis," a theme that has surely sustained more authors and screenwriters than any other typically modern narrative. In search of "freedom," "experience," and "meaning" (as well as a variety of adulterated pleasures) the hero/ine bites his or her lip and heads for points east, north, west, south—whichever way the Promise lies. And the Promise, always the same, is that, once loosed from the constraints of home and hometown, the protagonist will "find himself." True identity discovered: the flower blooms.

It is worth noting that in the British and American context the hero's quest does not start with leaving just any sort of town—it is usually launched from a Protestant- or Catholic-shaped town, fussy, hypocritical, and dull. Sherwood Anderson rendered with unmistakable disdain the life of one of these towns in his 1919 novel *Winesburg, Ohio*, a sort of midwestern *No Exit*. Winesburg was dusty, the locals estranged from each other, and vitality of any sort was absent. Given this sort of portrait, who wouldn't take the first train out? The Big City awaits, after all, modern, anonymous, forgiving. It may have taken a village to raise the young, but only by leaving the hometown and its debilitating ways can he or she be liberated, allowing the ideal self to emerge, enlightened and awake.

Of course, shifts in Western thinking can't alone account for the primacy of this freedom fable. Its plausibility was rooted in a new way of life, one that turned the household, once an economic unit in its own right, into mere sleeping quarters for kin who spent their days out building the modern world. Gradually kin became strangers. The more "progress" we made—wagons powered by engines, not horses; theater on screen, not in a hall; conversation through a wire, not over a table—the less we seemed to need each other, or even belong together. Such "progress" led to all relationships, even kinship relations, being founded, as the historian Christopher Shannon puts it, on "choice and consent," rather than on obligation, by then a dirty word. Being a parent became no more than a "role" one played, or opted not to play.

But one fact remains, whatever we imagine our "roles" to be: we *are* kin. This *is* our shape. And if kinship grounds our identity, then the fact that the guiding narratives of our time, as well as their supporting social and economic structures, work to dissolve them, is evidence that mischief at high levels has been taking place. It might even heighten our conviction that we need to relearn basic lessons about ourselves and who we were born to be. It's either that, or continue to usher in corruption, family by family, neighborhood by neighborhood, generation by generation.

A guide was sent to lead us out of this mess and take us home.

From the moment he began to speak publicly he seldom stopped giving himself titles that had to do with sonship. Queried at a young age about some deviant behavior, his disarming retort was, "I must be about my father's business." He often cast himself as a son, the son of a king, even, in stories of his own devising. This angered quite a few, but it entranced others. Who was this man of suspect origins who claimed to be "the Son"?

He never equivocated: he made it clear that he was speaking on behalf of his father. "I have come in my father's name," he said simply. Throughout a brief career that brought him both popularity and scorn, he found his center in his sense of sonship. "I live because of the father," he confessed in the synagogue one day.

His was no remote, evasive father. The son prayed, with what must have been quiet fervor, that his closest friends might know "the love with which you loved me." His was a father who gave to his son that which all children require: unmistakable, unmasked displays of paternal delight. "This is my beloved son, in whom I am well pleased!," the father thundered to a stunned crowd one day. Theirs was a love, it seems, that went both ways. It was a love that to our jaded eyes might even seem corny or posed—except for the deadly mission it was underwriting.

The father longed, the author of Hebrews explains, "to bring many sons to glory." This desire led to an extraordinary sacrifice and exchange: the abandoning of him who was most precious for the sake of those who were estranged. The prodigals would be brought back to the table. And so the Son made his way toward the cross, ever aware of the paternal blessing that was shaping him and guiding him.

To see ourselves as we are is to despair: we fail to be who we were intended to be, and nothing shows this more sharply than the quality of our kinship relations. But to catch a glimpse of Christ and his father is to gain hope: I am not stuck in this dismal state. One day I will become the son or daughter I was born to become.

When the apostle Paul glimpsed this prospect he spilled out his grandest passage of all. Creation may be groaning, he wrote, but someday we shall all be liberated. We will finally experience, together, "the glorious freedom of the children of God." Home at last.

Jesus, in a disturbing blanket statement, once matter-of-factly called his own followers "evil." "If you then, though you are evil, know how to give good gifts to your children, how much more will your father in heaven give good gifts to those who ask him!" "Good gifts": an irresistible offer. But what were these gifts? Later he cleared up the mystery at least a bit: the gift would be the Holy Spirit. He would come alongside, moving us, gently and persistently, toward home.

Maybe it was the King James English of my childhood that spawned the distorted images—actually, the flat-out fear—of this gift, this "counselor." *The Holy Ghost.* How could a ten-year-old not be spooked? Worse, frightening camp meetings led me to conclude that demonic possession and the spirit's filling were probably not all that different. I could not have been more wrong.

Demons take their eerie delights in loss, death, and destruction. They live to hollow out, to diminish that which is solidly good. And so far as they are concerned, we, their prey, are well on our way in the most desirable of directions. Augustine described his pre-conversion heart as "void of the solidity" for which he longed. "Without you," he confessed, "what am I to myself but a guide to my own destruction?" Cut off from God we live in a diabolically hollow state. Satan's legions declare open season on us; we declare open season on each other. We need help.

So the Holy Spirit was sent to aid us in this in-between time. The Spirit alone makes possible the reversal of corruption: a good gift indeed. Reversing the demonic lack of wholeness, the Spirit fills the aching void with real flesh, true humanity. Far from hollowing us out, the Spirit rebuilds us, imparting solidity. Slowly we are restored, slowly we regain our shape: we become what our forebears called "virtuous." Cicero understood virtue to be "a nature perfect in itself . . . wrought up to the most consummate excellence." Virtue, in this ancient tradition, accrues to those who over the course of time come to inhabit their intended form. It is all about restoration. We have departed from our original estate; a virtuous person is one who has achieved palpable progress toward reinhabiting it .

The path of virtue always leads directly home. As we deny ourselves and reach warmly towards our own, we gain the weightiness, the *gravitas*, that marks the virtuous life. We impart to those near us the life that alone makes both them and us solid, crucifying all the while the impulses to self-diminish, to self-destruct. Gradually, we become for others a foretaste of a new day, a hint of what is to come.

In Wendell Berry's phrase, we learn to "practice resurrection." Against all odds, we enact the restoration.

This hope of reunion and restoration, when the curse is lifted and all is made new, demands a commitment—yea, a fiery devotion—to a life of kinship and caretaking here and now. Apart from this strenuous ethic we can only anticipate more emptiness, more ennui, more of what the old sage called "vanity of vanities." Apart from this vision we are destined to retrace the tired steps of so many who have gone before us, not to mention those with whom we now walk.

Consider a recent *New Republic* essay entitled "Portable," in which a new mother shares with remarkable candor a troubling series of self-discoveries. Reared in LaPorte, Indiana, where "traditional family values were the norm," she, upon college graduation intended to leave her native state, yet she also desired to give her children the sort of childhood she remembered warmly. "I certainly wanted to have children, and it was my intention to bring them up as I had been brought up," she says, her mother having "devoted her life" to raising her four children by staying at home. After a few years in Washington, DC, she and her husband had their first child. At that point, as she puts it, "LaPorte came alive in my heart." But she then faced a series of difficult questions: would she return to the work she had come to love? Would the family budget be met if she decided to stay home? Would she, in short, remain "a daughter of LaPorte"?

She made the angst-ridden decision to keep her job, but after her child's birth the story took an unexpected turn, what she calls "the great surprise": "I discovered that I lacked the patience I thought I would have with an infant." To be sure, she dearly loved the child. Yet, she confesses, "when the time came to go back to work, I felt relief," mingled with anxiety about abandoning received notions of parenting and family.

Tellingly, the new mother found additional relief in a Peruvian neighbor, "Lucy," whom she employed to care for her child. "The remarkable thing," she writes, "was that my son, who usually cried when held by strangers, was content in Lucy's arms." Lucy, it became clear, was the real deal: "It is perfectly clear to me that he gets more from Lucy than I could give him if I were to stay home," she reflects. The crisis, then, came to a satisfactory resolution. Although she curiously admits that "It is hard to watch your child cling to another woman and cry when you come to take him home," she closes the piece with sprightly confidence: "The city *has* changed me, but I am a better woman and a better mother for it."

The formulaic feel of this post-Christian confession—ironically and uneasily in the lineage of Augustine's—powerfully reveals how deeply embedded this freedom myth truly is. And like all stories, this one is heading somewhere. Where?

I suggest that we Americans, religious and irreligious alike, are becoming a people with diminishing capacities for giving care—even (perhaps especially) to our own. We have depleted, in the swift passage of two or three generations, the caretaking stock that today we see mainly in folks of retirement age, or in those who come to us from lands that have maintained better than we the ancient arts and habits of caring.

We now see that, for all their faults, those now leaving us were, as a generation, committed to caring for us, their families. The ache we feel at their departure mingles with fear, for as they go we begin to sense the degree to which we have turned away from the legacy they tried to pass along to us—an imperfect legacy, but fruitful nonetheless. This helps to explain the general public's current fascination with anything pertaining to World War II, a trend powerfully exhibited by Tom Brokaw's bestsellers chronicling *The Greatest Generation*. Misled by our social institutions and our own malign propensities, we widened the famed "generation gap" just enough to keep their ethic from seeping into our souls and seizing control of our lives. We evaded their way, and now we wonder why, as we sheepishly take inventory of our own diminishing inner resources.

About four years ago my grandmother spent six weeks in Baltimore. Her sister's husband had been languishing in a hospital there, unable to pull through a bout with pneumonia. For a month and a half my grandmother and her sister walked daily from the hotel room to the hospital to care for the ailing man. In the course of that time they made but one trip home. They argued with doctors, befriended nurses, and watched television at night in a room with a single chair. The husband and brother-in-law they cared for eventually died of the illness, and the two women complained bitterly about what they believed was negligent treatment on his behalf. Grandma still talks often about the whole experience, years later. And every time I hear it, I'm reminded: this is a woman who knows no other life but caring for those around her.

Someday all too soon she'll be gone—they all will. Then what? Who will teach us to care? Have we listened closely enough to their whispers? Have we dared to look them in the eyes, to see the soft sparkle of habitual sacrifice? Is it possible that we can learn to give as they have given?

There is time. There is always time for this sort of movement, so long as God grants it. In fact, the only reason God grants time at all is for this one end: that we may come to love, him and those near to us.

Surely life finds its center in this caring. By it we gain a freedom deep and true, an identity, finally, firmly intact. With Augustine we cry, "Come Lord, stir us up and call us back, kindle and seize us, be our fire and our sweetness. Let us love, let us run." And father, bring us home. If it please you, soon.

—2000

Elusive Unity

FROM HIS YEARS AS a Wheaton College student in the 1930s, to his long tenure as a leading evangelical theologian and spokesman, to his death in 2003 at the age of ninety, Carl F. H. Henry proclaimed a single bold conviction that might be summarized thus: *Human history and hope center on the gospel of Jesus Christ, and evangelical Protestantism is its most faithful expression in our momentous times.*

For Christians, the first part of this claim remains unproblematic, of course. It's the second that even self-identifying evangelicals—let alone other Christians—may today find audacious. What, in twenty-first-century America, does it mean to be an "evangelical"? And could it possibly be that evangelical Protestantism, whatever it is, fares so favorably when placed alongside older, more sturdy incarnations of Christian faith? These days, many Protestants to the left and to the right of Henry have their doubts about the meaning and usefulness of the term "evangelical."

Henry didn't. He was self-conscious and confident in his use of it, and wore it with a sense of honor. Why?

What Henry in his 1986 autobiography called a mere "tract" is, as it turns out, the book he is best remembered by today, his 1947 work *The Uneasy Conscience of Modern Fundamentalism.* At the time, "fundamentalism" was not associated with Muslim terrorists, compound-dwellers, or even right-wing activists. Rather, it was the label attached to those early-twentieth-century Protestants who, in the face of the powerful arguments of modernist intellectuals, resolutely affirmed the central doctrines of the historic Christian faith. In what became known as the "fundamentalist-modernist controversy," these Protestants rallied together in an effort to preserve the orthodoxy of their particular denominations, as well as to safeguard the American republic itself. Despite their strenuous efforts—including a multivolume work called *The Fundamentals*, which featured essays from an interdenominational array of scholars and was mailed to *all* ministers in the United States— they failed spectacularly to achieve their main ecclesiastical and cultural aims.

Henry, born in 1913, was their admirer and heir. As a new convert he had witnessed in the 1930s and 40s the fundamentalists' declining academic, ecclesiastical, and cultural fortunes, and in *The Uneasy Conscience* he tried to call them back and push them forward. His book aggressively summoned conservatives, in the face of fragmentation within Protestantism and geopolitical catastrophe without, to embrace one another, along with the social implications of the gospel they confessed. "The time has come now for Fundamentalism to speak with an ecumenical outlook and voice," he insisted. "If it speaks in terms of the historic Biblical tradition, rather than in the name of secondary accretions or of eschatological biases on which evangelicals divide, it can refashion the modern mind."

It was a great hope, this vision of triumphal unity, and as he came into his own as an evangelical intellectual in the 1950s he continued to press for it, with the steady conviction that to fail to achieve this unity was to fail the gospel itself. Moving reluctantly in 1956 from his teaching post at Fuller Seminary to become the founding editor of *Christianity Today*, he effectively guided, at huge personal and scholarly costs, an effort to bring conservative Protestants—now called "evangelicals"— together once more.

The Dutch Calvinist theologian G. C. Berkouwer of the Free University of Amsterdam registered the mood of these men in the lead article of the inaugural issue when he declared that "the struggle around orthodoxy, which took such fierce form in the nineteenth century, is not a thing that belongs only to the past." It was this "struggle around orthodoxy" that they self-consciously joined, writing and thinking against the backdrop of a social crisis they believed to be rooted in the West's collective turning away from Christian faith. They joined hands, Protestants of many varieties, to face together a civilization whose most brilliant thinkers dismissed their way of seeing and thinking with little more than a scoff.

And so, crucially, for Henry and those near him the term "evangelical" had an extraverted, outward thrust: the "evangelical" endeavor was not centered on preaching to theological conservatives but rather on winning those beyond their borders. Being "evangelical" in Henry's mind was not about internal renewal so much as external thrust. He and his editorial cohort fashioned *Christianity Today* accordingly.

They were, in many respects, unimaginably successful. In his autobiography Henry modestly called their initial efforts "an impressive launch," and it was all of that and more. Following in the traces of the earlier fundamentalists, each biweekly issue of *CT* was sent to 160,000 Protestant ministers and seminary students (thanks to the generous patronage of Sun Oil magnate J. Howard Pew); at the end of the first year the number of paid subscriptions was at 38,000—some 4,000 beyond the total of their more established liberal rival, the *Christian Century*. Within a short time Henry was able to attract respected scholars and churchmen from outside of the evangelical orbit as occasional (and strategically useful) contributors; they joined an able cadre of evangelical writers to help establish the magazine and its constituency in the public eye.

That peculiar Protestant entity formerly known as "fundamentalism" had begun to speak with the "ecumenical outlook and voice" that Henry in *The Uneasy Conscience* had called for, and many took note. Henry's Fuller Seminary colleague and Old Testament scholar Gleason Archer spoke for many when in a letter to Henry in 1959 he opined, "Something is being done through your magazine which has not been done before in this century, and the whole Protestant scene in American has been profoundly affected by its astonishing success." By 1967 the magazine would reach a high of 163,000 paid subscribers, an enviable number by any standard, and Henry would be fully established as the leading intellectual of the movement.

He had his concerns—plenty of them, as his 1967 book *Evangelicals at the Brink of Crisis* makes clear. Published in the aftermath of the Berlin Conference on World Evangelism (sponsored by *CT* as part of what Henry called a "tenth anniversary project" and attracting some 1,100 delegates from more than 100 countries), the book expressed Henry's continued hope for a deepening evangelical ecumenism, centered on the evangelistic mission of the church. As usual, he spoke in a prophetic voice: "If evangelical Christians do not join heart to heart, will to will, and mind to mind across their multitudinous fences, and do not deepen their loyalties to the Risen Lord of the Church, they may well become—by the year 2000—a wilderness cult in a secular society with no more public significance than the ancient Essenes in the Dead Sea caves. In either event the tragic suppression of the evangel would abandon modern civilization to the new Dark Ages."

Henry's sense of looming crisis was prescient. It's no coincidence that in the 1970s his influence began to crest as the shape of evangelicalism, and America itself, shifted in ways that impeded the sort of unity, identity, and confidence that he for more than three decades had been working to forge—an identity grounded in the conviction that to be "evangelical" was the most important identifier any Christian could embrace.

One crisis he did not foresee was his forced exit from the magazine in 1968, a circumstance that to this day remains mysterious. As he began work on long-delayed scholarly projects, he watched, more remotely now, as evangelicals reasserted themselves in increasingly boisterous, sometimes impressive ways: the rise of a Christian Left, the rise of a Christian Right, the rise of a Christian recording industry, the rise of a Christian College Coalition, and the rise of countless new evangelical churches, parachurch agencies, and media outlets.

It was remarkable growth, to be sure. But was it the sort of unified front Henry had hoped for? Not exactly—as indicated by the fact that many of those rising were decidedly ambivalent about his pioneering efforts.

Some baby boomers coming of age in the 1960s and 70s criticized his politics as too conservative, inadequately responsive to matters of race, class, gender, and political economy. For others, Henry was not conservative enough: too much regard for the state, too tolerant of ideological diversity, too cautious in his treatment of issues like abortion (he granted what in 1982 he termed "an ethical basis for voluntary abortion in cases of incest and rape"). To the next generation, Henry had become the "careful moderate," in political scientist Robert Booth Fowler's words, acknowledged as a "trailblazer" and then pushed to the side. Fracturing left and right, evangelicals reflected the broader political divisions that convulsed the country as the Cold War's political and cultural consensus collapsed. The era of "culture wars" was underway. But the political disputes among evangelicals in the 1970s and 80s dim alongside the heavy theological combat that was being joined.

The "Battle for the Bible" among evangelicals again turned Henry into the man in the middle, clinging needlessly to the outmoded doctrine of inerrancy according to some scholars, while insufficiently combative in his public defense of it according to others. Reflecting years later on his work at *CT*, he recalled that "At no time during my editorship did we escalate the doctrine of inerrancy into a test of evangelical *authenticity*." Yearning for an elusive evangelical unity, he continued to maintain, as he hopefully put it in 1987, that "a basic theological consensus survives," centered on "the self-revealing God and Christ's gospel authorized by inspired Scripture." This, for him, was the core of evangelical identity.

But was it identity enough? By the 1990s doubts about the desirability of Henry's vision of a robust evangelical ecumenism were mounting on all sides. As American public life fractured into identity politics, evangelicals likewise became more attuned to their particular ecclesiastical and theological traditions. These explorations of ecclesiastical identity are seen nowhere more clearly than in a 1991 book published by InterVarsity Press, *The Varieties of Evangelicalism*, in which scholars from twelve distinct American Protestant traditions weighed and measured the relationship of their traditions with evangelicalism. The mid-century evangelical coalition, upon closer examination, began to look Reformed to some, at the exclusion of Wesleyans, Pentecostals, and African-American denominations of various sorts. Ironically, for some confessional Presbyterians, evangelicalism, far from being Reformed, had become an unwitting carrier of the demons of modernity. For the sake of the survival of their own tradition, these conservatives urged near-total separation from it.

In short, the popular image of evangelicals in the 1980s and 90s as a powerful electoral force and consumer bloc was accurate only from a distance. Closer examination revealed that behind the seemingly united front were division, diversity, and disunity, produced by powerful centrifugal forces. At its best, this moment of confused resurgence spawned serious searching for historical and communal depth; at its worst, it yielded an all-too-familiar shallowness and cynicism, born of the deadly failure to achieve, both within and among the varying denominations and organizations, unity and depth. For many observers, the crisis that Henry had long prophesied had arrived.

This era that followed the collapse of the Cold War consensus we refer to today, clumsily, as "postmodernity," a time when most traditional forms of union and wholeness—whether civilizations, nations, religions, or genders—have come under radical attack at all levels. Given the atmospheric conditions, it's far from surprising that scholars, activists, and ordinary citizens have directed the same sort of searching suspicion at evangelicalism as they have at the nation itself. In many respects, it deserves it.

Like so many evangelicals of his generation and older, Henry tended to take for granted the ability of Christians to achieve a high, healthy level of communal thickness irrespective of creed, confession, or geographical location. Failing adequately to grasp the historically contingent nature of the communal elements—the practices, rituals, social structures—that Christian formation requires, he relied too heavily on the ecclesial elevation of Scripture alone to forge Christian communities. Yes, as he put it in 1957, "the awareness of biblical revelation as relevant to the whole of life grants contemporary civilization the living prospect of a rationally satisfying explanation of human aspirations and problems." But how do we *live*, day to day, this "rationally satisfying explanation"?

This is the sort of question we today find ourselves facing again and again. We long for the kind of cultural and communal richness, rooted deeply in the past, that might shape us into a people able to keep the faith, and keep it well, in these daunting times. Henry's generation sought this richness in the restoration of what they thought of as "Western civilization." Fifty years later, we know that such restoration was but a dream, and, as our continual quests for "community" attest, we struggle to fill this void that feels increasingly deep and dark.

Is it possible that evangelicalism as a religious tradition is somehow *responsible* for a measure of our malaise? Perhaps. The spiritual and theological vitality that evangelicals like Henry have called for may actually, in a sad irony, be at odds with the grand vision they promote. Put simply, the histories of our race reveal that unity, whether in families, nations, or churches, only becomes durable and sound when, paradoxically, it honors the personal and communal particularity that is always present when humans flourish. To the extent that evangelicals have pushed to the side the healthy ecclesiastical and theological particularities of their constituents, to that extent they may have damaged the very elements deep catholicity requires. On this view, evangelicalism, with its tendency to issue simplifying calls to unity, may be as much a dissolver of traditions as a tradition in its own right.

But if in our day we have discovered the need for particularity, surely, as the fracturing around us continues, we are rediscovering that particularity alone leaves us incomplete, that we cannot abide the absence of a unity deep and true. We, broken creatures of God, were made for wholeness, a wholeness woven with care from the delicate fabric of our personal and communal identities.

What is the church to be if not the agency and foretaste of this wholeness? Seen from this vantage, at its best evangelicalism reflects the wholesome catholic impulses of each of our not-so-discrete Christian traditions: the yearning of true believers across these temporal divisions for the unity for which Christ himself prayed—a unity always beyond our reach, yet necessary all the same.

Some are called to serve the cause of unity, others the work of building particular communions. Few in the history of American Protestantism have served the cause of unity so well as Carl Henry. By urging Christians to wage together what he once termed the "age-old battle against unbelief," he called us to a present and future catholicity premised on the sovereign rule of the Son of God: the beneficent King of a realm that will, one day, be unified on earth as it is in heaven. There are worse visions to champion.

—2004

Broken Man

DISCOVERING MARK HEARD IN the late 1980s was like mainlining hope itself. DJs on Christian radio stations rarely played the music of the man whom Bruce Cockburn would call America's best singer-songwriter. He didn't sing much about his "walk," or about "reaching out," or even about Jesus. No, he spoke of "red fires of war," and some "threat of annihilation" that "pounds at your door." No wonder I only heard him occasionally.

After my college years, in the midst of an aching search for something deep enough to sustain my shredded faith, I bought a best-of collection of Heard's acoustic songs. Never since has such a small investment yielded such amazing returns. His wedding in word and melody of raw confession, revealing observation, and restless probing far surpassed anything I had ever encountered by a Christian artist.

I was immediately in his debt, and Matthew Dickerson's book about Heard, *Hammers and Nails*, reveals that debtors like me abound. Crafted more as a mosaic than as a textured biography, it offers an unprecedented chance to peer into the life of a man who displayed a rare and beautiful vulnerability, song after song. Crucially, the story Dickerson tells has significance beyond the life of one musician. If the intersection of art, theology, and the market has any bearing on the future of Christianity in America, believers of all varieties will find something instructive, and perhaps ominous, in this story.

Born in Macon, Georgia, in 1951, Heard, we discover, was picking out songs on a piano before he was four. By the time he entered college at the University of Georgia he had found his way to the guitar and to Christ, writing original music for his band and edging toward the Jesus Music scene.

His music bore the imprint of the era—country-tinged folk in the singer-songwriter vein—while his nascent faith was distinctively Southern and evangelical. In key respects, his life by his mid-twenties had become a quest to transcend these worlds, while somehow staying true to what they at their best were. After hearing Francis Schaeffer speak at a Presbyterian church in Macon in 1975, Heard, like so many others of his generation and disposition, ventured to Switzerland and L'Abri in the hope that he might find answers to his deepening questions, and perhaps join his faith and art in a more satisfying way.

The long and costly sojourn Heard began that year turned out to be a rough one, as this book amply shows, but his life-long musical and lyrical record of it is a treasure. Heard's experience at L'Abri, intensive throughout the 1970s, gave him a counterpoint of near-salvific value to an evangelical Christianity that, he was discovering, had little ability to nurture him and his art. Still, he found himself wedded to that subculture (he called it "the ghetto") through the auspices of two CCM record companies.

In the course of making seven albums for them between 1978 and 1985 he won the respect of critics but little favor from record buyers. Dickerson's interviews mesh with Heard's lyrics and liner notes to reveal a man striving energetically, often angrily, to make contact with a world that couldn't fathom him: when he sang about his own life the theme was often not triumph but anguish; when he turned his gaze toward the world he spoke, sometimes awkwardly, a language of social criticism that sounded alien alongside the lyrical fare of Amy Grant, Leon Patillo, and the other evangelical celebrities of the era.

In the mid-1980s Heard made a quick exit from the CCM scene. Without a record contract himself, he produced records for other artists, performed occasionally, and kept making music. Finally in 1990 he established his own label, Fingerprint Records, and released three albums that were, in a word, stunning; one critic went so far as to posit that, "Arguably, no artist has crafted three consecutive albums with both the lyrical radiance and the musical vibrancy to rival *The Dry Bones Dance, Second Hand*, and *Satellite Sky*." As he was nearing an agreement with a mainstream label in 1992 he died at the age of forty, after suffering two heart attacks.

By the time he recorded his last three records the dense brilliance of his art crowned a pilgrimage of unusual intensity, honesty, intelligence, and pain. On his last record he describes himself as a "broken man . . . outcast on the outskirts of the promised land"—a poignant evocation of his bewildered disappointment at so many levels. But he goes on in the album's last song to steer the listener toward another lonely place, where triumph mingles always with pain.

> I saw the city at its tortured worst
> And you were outside the walls there
> You were relieved of a lifelong thirst
> I was dry at the fountain
> I knew that you could see my shame
> But you were eyeless and sparing
> I awoke when you called my name
> I felt the curtain tearing

It's a fitting final confession for a man who sought above all to help us to be *true*. Of his many gifts to us, this was his greatest. Fortunately for us, it's a gift that keeps on giving. Maybe some day we'll receive it.

—2003

Free Indeed?

THE LAND OF THE Free, it turns out, has been rough on people seeking freedom, including evangelicals. Torn between competing visions of freedom, visions we evangelicals helped cast long ago, we wander this way and that, now stumbling, now running, heedless and hesitant, trying like good Americans, like good Christians, just to be free at last. Free indeed.

Not that we usually see ourselves so clearly. But our quandary comes out, and sometimes in strange ways—none stranger than the recent rise of Amish fiction, where earnest romance writing draws readers into worlds at once familiar and alien. Stories of girls sweating Julys away in layers of dark fabric, boys fumbling for words behind trotting horses, have entranced us by the tens of thousands. One leader of the scribbling pack, Beverly Lewis, has become a *New York Times* bestselling author with titles like *The Englisher* and *The Brethren*. While some evangelicals thrill to visions of a planet Left Behind, others are looking wistfully behind, to a world that's refused to simply go along with it all, the mad dash to freedom be damned.

I used to live among the Amish. I can relate. I was in graduate school then, and my wife and I were living in Lancaster County, Pennsylvania, the parents of two small boys. A few times a week I drove down aged roads to a university as distant from all the Amish embodied as one could fathom. At least once a week, usually while pushing a stroller or taking a run alongside Amish farms, I was tempted to give up and join in. I mentioned this once to a neighbor, the daughter of an "English" (as the Amish refer to the non-Amish) family, beekeepers, that belonged to our large, suburban Presbyterian church. She immediately nodded her head in agreement.

In those days I would drive by a house and see five or six wheelchairs in a circle on the lawn of the family caring for the handicapped of the neighborhood. And I'd look at our own jam-packed, lonely, high-tech life, and sigh. Make no mistake: the allure is real, and it's rooted in a sound intuition: that freedom means order, an order beyond the harum-scarum pace of the freeway, beyond the noise of our little digital jukeboxes.

But the writers of Amish fiction are not simply wistful. They are also critical—severely so, at times. There's a reckoning taking place in their stories, by way of a familiar conundrum the writers see writ large among the Amish. It might be summed up by the following question: when does law cease to be freedom's friend and become its enemy?

It's a question Americans, and American evangelicals in particular, have never quite made up their minds about. Is the Land of the Free really kind to freedom? Or does it tend to thwart it?

A century ago, as this new, liberal rendition of Western civilization was being erected, the astute German social philosopher Max Weber famously called it an "iron cage," despite its evident, emerging liberties. The Amish said "no thanks," ducking out as the cage went up. A century later, evangelicals, among others, wander back, peering through the bars, trying to figure out who's on the outside and who's on the inside. If these books are any indication, it's no easy task.

To Cindy Woodsmall, the matter is clear: the Amish embody not freedom but bondage—stony orthodoxy, cold hearts. In the end, their elaborate guarding of the Christian faith reduces it, as her narrator in *When the Heart Cries* puts it, to "adherence to rules."

Woodsmall wastes no time with pleasantries. No sooner does her Amish protagonist, seventeen-year-old Hannah Lapp, accept a marriage proposal from a Mennonite boy she's secretly seeing than she ends up being raped by an Englisher driving down her lane. It makes for a rough first chapter. As the story unfolds, it's clear that for Woodsmall what Hannah needs is what her whole community needs: to embrace a freer faith, one more personal, spiritual, biblical. In short, they need to become evangelicals. Hannah's fiancé, trying to understand this trapped community, has already been given eyes to see; Hannah "fell into guilt far too effortlessly" thanks to her formation within a world of "rigid repression." But through her ordeal, Hannah discovers something precious and wonderful, revealed in a prayer her brother, amid his own spiritual awakening, cries out: "There's a part of You that talks to people sometimes. That tells us something that isn't passed down by the church leaders . . . or *Daed* [Dad]."

Lewis tries the Amish on the same charges in her Heritage of Lancaster County series, centered on identity crises of varying levels. When Katherine discovers that she was not born in the Amish community but adopted into it at a young age, her spirit soars—at times. But at no time higher than when she, having left the community, visits a relative's less constrained, more modern Mennonite church. As the congregation rises to sing, Lewis writes, "all heaven came down, pouring right in through the lovely, bright windows. A foretaste of glory filled the place." Free at last.

The part Mennonites play in these two stories is instructive. Placed at the nexus between Amish rigidity and American anarchy, they illumine the underlying effect the Amish have on the evangelical imagination, whatever overt antagonism these writers feel toward what they believe is a misguided, even counterfeit Christianity. Despite their wrongheaded radicalism, Lewis and friends know, the Amish are doing *something* right.

Not all the writers see the Amish in such a harsh light. Wanda Brunstetter, author of the Brides of Lancaster County series, skips the Mennonite middle ground entirely, happy to turn the Amish themselves into her ideal Christian community. In her Amish world, warm piety and sound theological sense rule. Her plain people live in an Amish Mayberry, at a charmed distance from the "troublesome, hectic modern world," as bride Miriam sees it.

Struggling with bitterness over disappointed love, Miriam has the good fortune to belong to a community that surrounds her with loving admonition. "You don't seem to be as interested in spiritual things as you should," her suitor is compelled to tell her, echoing the concerns of others. Yet he persists: "I believe we can work through your bitterness together." Here the deeply communal Amish, heirs of the sixteenth-century Radical Reformation, draw wandering believers back to the ancient, early church root.

Real freedom doesn't come easily for anyone, of course—no not one, no matter the civilization, nation, or faith. The soul longs for freedom and knows somehow that it comes by love, and the best stories show the wonder of this union. "The single desire that dominated my search for delight," wrote Augustine of Hippo in *The Confessions*, "was simply to love and be loved."

We evangelicals, with deep pietistic roots that emerge from the Augustinian trunk, are not for nothing called exponents of the "religion of the heart." We understand freedom to be the fruit of an experiential, intensely personal faith. We believe that order, while necessary, must serve this end—and we tend to assume that traditional ecclesial and theological forms of order have not done so.

If these writers find fault with the Amish on this count—order gone bad—it has a lot to do with their own stories. A half-century ago, American evangelicals themselves were bound to a strict, idiosyncratic code, one that after the 1960s many evangelicals came to see as legalistic, a core element of the fundamentalism (as they still called it) that had lost sight of freedom itself. If the Amish fiction phenomenon shines light on any chapter of recent evangelical history, it's the jagged, uncertain walk of many baby boomers, in this free-form, postmodern moment, from fundamentalism to what we think of today as evangelicalism.

In light of this odyssey, a palpable ambivalence toward what the Amish represent is to be expected. After Woodsmall's protagonist, Hannah, spends long days in a hospital caring for a friend, she begins to see that the nurses "didn't hang on what men thought or wanted, not like she had." Woodsmall, wisely, grants that a real deepening of common understanding has taken place in at least some areas of contemporary American life, including the confusing realm of gender.

But the older world still speaks powerfully. Hannah, struggling to understand her own ambivalence toward her native community, is touched at a crucial moment by "the tenderness of those who had known her all her life—who knew her mother, grandmother, and even her great-grandmother." And this tenderness "melted the edges of ice that had formed around her heart." The loyalty, the fidelity, the willed innocence of the Amish are noble, we are shown. But for freedom to ensue, they need a complement. For Woodsmall and Lewis, this complement comes compliments of American evangelicalism—dual, dueling identities, deeply enmeshed.

For all these authors' focus on the Amish, there's not a whole lot of evidence of a searching study of them, not of the sort serious fiction at least would require. At their worst, the writers seem to turn to the Amish in an opportunistic fashion, as an adequately alien, adequately familiar community they can use to imaginatively work out persisting cultural and theological questions.

Careless use of a subject is, of course, a familiar pop culture dynamic—how many movies set in the past take the audience no further into it than yesterday's newspaper? But this doesn't obviate the fact that artistic misrepresentation, even when the genre isn't expected to honor high standards of accuracy, is still at some level an injustice. So to what extent have these writers gotten the Amish right?

That's a question for scholars of Amish Christianity to take up. But another world of Amish fiction exists that might help us begin to answer this question. For the evangelical writers have in their midst an actual Amish writer who publishes with a small house in Lancaster named Good Books, more famous for its cookbooks than its fiction. If Linda Byler's work continues, though, that may change. *When Strawberries Bloom* bobs along with a comic touch, a story written by a true insider who knows what it's like to grow up caring for horses and eating Amish food and navigating the *English* world. In Byler's hands, we glimpse what it might actually feel like to be Amish and feel free.

Byler's protagonist, Lizzie Glick, is charmingly drawn, a spunky, impulsive, innocently fickle young woman trying to make sense of love, life, and faith within the bounds of an enduring and demanding tradition. Happily, it's a tradition that comes across as strange, in the best sense; in a few places the book has the feel of a translation. Yet Glick's is also a familiar world. Learning to embrace "the will of God," central throughout the book, is of course a primary aspiration among evangelicals, having a common formation by the language of Scripture (though the communal obligations the Amish believe manifest this embrace will no doubt seem confining to many evangelicals).

Points of distant connection between the Amish and American evangelicals extend in many directions, it turns out. We learn that some Amish use Betty Crocker cookbooks, make pizza, and read Laura Ingalls Wilder (whom Lizzie turns to in a failed effort to persuade her parents to put up a Christmas tree). Amish girls too puzzle over their wardrobe selections, and their families stress the desirability of "a clean and honorable courtship." But then there is this revealing fact: Amish newlyweds in Byler's community don't move into their own house until several weeks following their wedding, after they've had time to visit all who attended the extensive wedding festivities. It's within their guests' homes that they receive their wedding gifts.

Byler's story is a romance, to be sure, a graceful celebration of Amish life. But more deeply, it's a celebration of life itself, absent the melodrama of the other stories. A comic vision guides Byler's narrative, in which reconciliation and union are the final, unmerited, blessed end. The Amish *Ordnung,* the code that governs life together, here turns out to be not a cage but a pathway, leading to a distinct kind of freedom: peculiar, out of fashion, but real nonetheless, and successful at repelling many of the toxins that survey after survey show have poisoned evangelical families and churches.

It's not just evangelicals who find themselves mysteriously drawn to the Amish these days. Steven Stoll, a leading environmental historian, concludes his landmark book, *Larding the Lean Earth: Soil and Society in Nineteenth Century America,* with an admiring visit to an Amish community. Kentucky writer and farmer Wendell Berry has long lauded the Amish as moral exemplars of the most impressive kind, describing their tradition as "solid enough to build a civilization upon"—an enviable judgment, to say the least, as we the free watch families, neighborhoods, topsoil, and mountaintops being washed to the sea.

Does it mean something that fifty-something church ladies are reading Amish fiction at the same time that twenty-something evangelical hipsters are reading Wendell Berry? Is this the immaturity of nostalgia? Or the intelligence of hope?

I think it's a good deal of the latter. Or at least I hope it is. In Lancaster we lived one mile from the now famous West Nickel Mines School, where in the fall of 2006 a troubled Englisher shot ten Amish girls, killing five and himself. The community's response touched the world with a witness rarely seen, and nearly impossible to understand: they forgave. Is there greater evidence of freedom?

—2010

In Search of Faces, Books, Friends

WE TWENTY-FIRST-CENTURY AMERICANS, PARTICIPANTS in an unending and unrelenting technological revolution, now find ourselves living through what future generations will no doubt remember as the Facebook Revolution. This has in turn ushered in the Facebook Inquisition, which empowers citizens everywhere to challenge the recalcitrant with a single daunting question: *why aren't you on it?*

I confess: I am not now, nor have I ever been, a Facebook user, much less a Facebook "friend." Even as most earthlings under the age of seventy have now joined this new communion of saints, I have resisted that upward call, and intend to persist in my rebellion. Mom, Dad, brothers and sisters, friends and neighbors, here's why:

1. I already have too many "friends" and too few *friends*.

2. Must we now do everything by screen—nature, entertainment, education, play, the weather, music, pets, maps, the news, correspondence, dating, gambling? Putting all of life on screen is starting to carry the sinister scent of tyranny, and look like the screening of reality itself. For my own self-understanding, protection, and enrichment, I need the world direct.

3. My best chance for satisfaction is where *I* live—not where you live. And it's certainly not in that netherworld known as the Internet. If I really find myself living, it will be because I'm living *here*—not as a voyeur craving other places, faces, and times.

4. Addiction and depression go together. I already know too much of the latter and many studies show a sharp rise in the former, especially connected to online activities.

5. What does our always-online way of life actually cost? Outrage over ecological degradation coupled with an easy embrace of the next electrical dependency is a tortured pairing—and it's all too familiar.

6. Facebook culture is helping to erode the received meanings—and thus experience—of three treasured words: *face, book, friend*. The first is one of the most beautiful, miraculous gifts. The second is an already perfected cultural achievement. The third is the anchor of life itself.

7. "Social networking" and neighborliness are at enmity. The former is the creation of a self-selected, self-celebrating circle of those who are instrumentally useful. The latter honors—indeed, prefers—those who happen into our worlds without invitation. The Good Samaritan was no "social networker." He was a neighbor. And he saved lives.

8. Must we really embrace everything "they" roll out? The simple ability to refuse is an all-too-necessary virtue in our glutted age.

9. I will not submit the complexity of my life to a medium and culture that will relentlessly simplify it, pressuring me to turn my life, day after day, into the spiritual equivalent of a greeting card. I have no desire to mislead anyone—but especially not myself—about the sadness and joy that make up my life.

10. The God of my faith didn't send pictures. And he wasn't satisfied with alphabets. In his economy, the word *had* to become flesh.

11. It's you I miss—your eyes, your face, your voice. And if I can't be with you, please, send your hand. It's the handwritten letters from my parents that I keep in my bed stand that give solace and hope on lonely nights.

Can't you see? It's *you* I need—unscreened. Come, eat my food, drink my wine, stay the night. Just come.

—2009

Vacationing with the Pagans

THE BEATLES? THEY WERE the creepy guys with stringy hair and granny glasses to my wife and me, children of the seventies. But they're groovy once more, and our fourteen-year-old son loves them. So we draft along in his excitement and head to the Beatles concert in Virginia Beach.

It is July 4, and we're on vacation. "The Beatles" aren't. This version of the fab four goes by the name Revolution and makes (one imagines) a pretty good living doing dead-on covers of Beatles songs, complete with wigs and changes of costume that go from the sleek thin-tie look of the early sixties to the sunburst radiance of the late sixties. The resemblance of "John" to John is particularly uncanny, even eerie, but George's hairpiece is awful. Ringo's "With a Little Help from My Friends" rings true, if a bit heavy. Paul is bright, light, young, and magnetic. He even plays left-handed bass.

It works. The crowd, the Atlantic Ocean to its back, chants and sways. The evening begins with sunshiny harmonies, Sinatra, Como, and Cole not so far away. It ends with Lucy in the sky with diamonds imagining there's no heaven, guitars unshackled, voices unthrottled, the crowd swept into another summer of love, guided, indeed, through a revolution—as true a revolution as we in our time have known.

I watch. My son joins in.

The distance between "I Want to Hold Your Hand" and "I Am the Walrus" seems inexplicable. How do you move in less than four years from touching innocence to existential absurdity?

These guys do it every night in two hours. From the start the crowd knows what's coming: the sweet chirpy harmonies are only preparing the way for the raw intensity of Real Rock and Roll, the unleashed in-exorable electronic rush that will crash like a train across the landscape. The dancing changes as the train draws near. A dark, shirtless baby boomer with a long face and ponytail emerges from somewhere in the crowd; he turns his body into a rhythmic swirling mass and becomes for a moment the new cynosure. As if on cue, many in the crowd begin to point devices at him, recording his performance, on their faces a familiar mixture of appreciation and amusement. *Who is this guy? Ah— the guy who shows up at every concert I've ever been to.*

When the Sergeant Pepper transformation begins the number standing at the stage triples and all manner of manic activity breaks out. My wife and I notice (what she calls) "the bouncing girls," a pair of pretty teenagers, a blond and brunette, who, seized by the spirit, enact the famed psychadelic rhythms with enormous infectious creativity, bending, swaying, entwining with shrieking serpentine delight. They bounce from the right side of the stage to the center, directly beside our son. He's so taken with the music he barely notices them (or so he says).

This concert, compressing the Beatles' lifespan into one short evening (yet somehow giving it the feeling of eternity), makes it clear that in the 1960s an encompassing tautness, a still lingering tension, was swiftly and permanently eased, neckties turned magically to tie-dye. Tightness, once the friend, quickly became the enemy; flowers, formerly dainty, now had power. We began to *rock!*

What do the Beatles stand for if not this change?

What *happened?* What does it mean?

All kinds of names have been given to this transformation. But this concert leaves me thinking one thought: *We're on vacation with the new pagans. They're everywhere.*

Paganism: an old word with enduring resonance, and for good reason. Think of it as the state of heart and mind that has emerged as the reality of Law has come, over the past century, to seem less and less real—a long historical process that reached a kind of climax in the six-ties, when to "question authority" meant, among other things, to ques-tion the very existence of authority.

Crucially, though, among the varying norms and mores Americans challenged were many that reflected misguided perceptions of Law, often rooted in the idiosyncratic culture of American Protestantism. In the sixties' aftermath these received ideas, on matters ranging from hair length to alcohol to race relations to worship, fell quickly. Vast space opened up in which efforts could be made to (re)define freedom, authority, and Law.

This chaotic, intoxicating sense of new space is what marked the seventies, and it extended right into the heart of the evangelical world. The "biblical" warrant that had once helped sustain Jim Crow, for instance, suddenly became an embarrassment. Perhaps even more telling was the 1976 publication of *The Act of Marriage,* the fundamentalist pastor Timothy LaHaye and his wife Beverly's surprisingly graphic answer to the considerably more graphic *The Joy of Sex*, published in 1972. The times certainly were "a-changin'," and with it the old-time religion itself.

Forty years on, it's possible to appreciate more fully what has— shall we say—"been goin' on." The moral direction and tension the Law had long foisted on Western civilization has by our day nearly vanished. With the sweeping away over the past century of innumerable small-L laws came the overarching dismissal of Law itself. A recognizably Christian culture has given way to a new paganism. What is this?

It is the embrace of nature without Nature. It is the reverence of *bios*, physical life, in tandem with a dimming awareness of *zoe*, spiritual life. It is, in fact, the mistaking of physical life *for* spiritual life, with all the historically ingrained religious sensibilities rushing toward *bios* with a very familiar zeal.

So now, for us twenty-first-century pagans, being twenty-five is all—the most alive we'll ever be. Men and women on both sides of that envied age try with holy fervency to attain it, whatever the cost in dollars or dignity. The hair must be cut just so (and then cut again and again—just so). The body must be kept trim, ever prepared for a twenty-five-year-old's feats. Old age never looked so bad. What red-blooded American male today would ever want to wake up and find himself married to a *grandmother*? What American woman wants to *look* like one?

It all adds up to a great calamity, no? But if so, why do even the most holy among us don tie-dye now and then?

Clearly, for all their standard bemoaning of the fate of America after the sixties, evangelicals have in evident ways embraced the profound changes in sensibility, style, and thought the era brought—and often with good reason. Even paganism, it turns out, has redemptive worth.

In an essay on the Christian poet W. H. Auden, Alan Jacobs helps us to see this possibility more clearly. Jacobs notes that in the middle decades of the twentieth century Auden came to reject the assumption, pervasive in Protestantism, that "our life in nature is at best an embarrassment," that God saves us to help us transcend the earth. On the contrary, Auden sensed, an embrace of our materiality seemed paradoxically to be what spiritual health required: a basic, primordial acknowledgement that we are not gods but *creatures* of God, living as biological beings under his reign.

Auden understood, in short, that the necessary response to our finitude is not the rejection of the material order but rather the reverent celebration of it. And it is this affirmation that Christians have been, over the centuries, prone to neglect or reject, right down to our times. To put it sharply: if there is a new paganism pervading America, we American Protestants have had a hand in preparing the way for it. In cultivating a spirituality that neglected the human, the earthy, the sensual, we fostered—in diabolical irony—a conceit that taught us to see ourselves as *superior* to our bodies, as well as the earth, regarding them as at best a species of a finitude that will, gratefully, some day pass.

But we are not superior to our bodies, nor the earth. In fact, we don't deserve them. And, fortunately, as Scripture teaches, we will never lose them.

Our too-spiritual spirituality ended up leaving us, as Christians but also as a wider populace, in considerable confusion about all things material, whether bathing suits or beer or bombs. And our disregard of the physical was bound to invite a walloping counter-embrace of it. By the sixties paganism was, once more, unshackled. Our creaturely identity, in all its post-edenic glory and corruption, became impossible to box in. The body was back.

A study of history certainly reveals the race's bipolar tendencies, as we swing back and forth between the enervating extremes of materiality and spirituality. The calling of Christians is to live at the point of tension between these poles, at the difficult but satisfying place that reveals the pathway to human flourishing, and leads others to it.

How can we get there? How can we stay?
The answer might be through worship.

All religious gatherings end with a kick, if they're any good. And Revolution is good. As the concert builds toward its climax John moves to the keyboard. The Bics flick on, flames swaying as arms extend toward the heavens, sea breeze an incense to savor. The hymn, so familiar, had to come, and it rings out, prophetic. "Imagine all the people/living for today . . ."

If only we *could* live, today or any day. If only we could pour our longings for life into each others' hearts and watch them blossom. If only our desires could be satisfied with good things, renewing our youth like the eagle's.

Forty years past Woodstock, this much is clear: our fevered yearning for vitality, this paganism, has its place. And its place is within the church. "The outer ring of Christianity," wrote G. K. Chesterton in *Orthodoxy*, one hundred years ago, "is a rigid guard of ethical abnegations and professional priests; but inside that inhuman guard you will find the old human life dancing like children, and drinking wine like men; for Christianity is the only frame for pagan freedom."

His next sentence is as chilling as the previous is warming: "But in the modern philosophy the case is the opposite; it is its outer ring that is obviously artistic and emancipated; its despair is within."

The lives of Chesterton's countrymen, the Beatles, born just a few years after his death, would become an emblem of this dynamic, this despair. Imagining there's no heaven didn't get them very far, it turns out, whatever the masses and marketers say today.

There are other things to imagine. One of them is a church whose worship flows from the beauty of creation, inspired not by Rock Band but by the Maker's hand, from he who fashioned majesty from clay, who sang us into our creaturely existence and who acts now to guide us back into it.

You may say that I'm a dreamer.
I am. And I'm not the only one.

—2009

Afterword

Epiphanies of Gratitude

I WAS IN THE midst of big changes that spring of 1981 when we piled into our chaperones' cars and headed to the *chapada* for our annual retreat.

The "we" was the student body of a high school in Cuiabá, Brazil, owned and operated by Wycliffe Bible Translators. The *chapada* is the towering plateau that encircles the large basin in which Cuiabá is located, an old western mining town founded during an early-eighteenth-century gold rush, now ballooned to a half-million inhabitants.

We students, all children of missionaries, came to a grand total of seven; the chaperones may have outnumbered us. Five of us were freshmen, including me. My family had just landed in Brazil the previous summer; the other students had lived in Brazil most of their lives. I was the newcomer, and, indeed, it was all new to me.

How to explain the wonder I felt as we lugged our gear down massive steps carved out of rock and I saw for the first time our destination? It was a clearing in the *mato* (not quite jungle, but almost) at the foot of a waterfall, some twenty feet wide and seventy-five or so feet below the dirt lot where we had parked. In the 1990s the area would become almost completely commercialized, but twenty years ago it was as pristine a spot as one could imagine a car being able to get to. A smaller waterfall was hidden a few hundred yards away from the one we camped beside, and a massive and majestic postcard-worthy waterfall tumbled over a huge cliff a couple miles away, the *Véu de Noiva* ("bridal veil"). It was an area rich in beauty. (And so, of course, rich in potential for "development"—my oldest sons now jockey over who gets to wear the camouflage *Chapada Dos Guimarães* t-shirt their grandparents brought home this year.)

Our gang set up headquarters beneath a rustic pavilion with a thatched roof, and someone started a fire for our opening night *churrasco*, the Brazilian-style barbeque that is the country's signature meal, on the same plane as *samba, futebol,* and *Carnaval.* The guys (four of us) set out to find a cluster of trees suitable for stringing up our hammocks. We slept under brilliant starry skies those nights, with the roar of the waterfall in the background and who knows what treacherous animals and insects nearby. My friends didn't seem to care, so I easily brushed my fears aside.

It was all too grand for me to grasp, and this trip was turning out to be the most magical experience yet of a ten-month odyssey that had left me breathless. I loved *futebol.* I loved my new friends. I loved life. Any country that could pull off something like the *chapada* was OK with me. I drank it in with a gusto I would not have believed myself to be capable of just one year before. All of this was, I knew full well, a gift.

I'm not sure how the giver of these gifts felt about the *Simon and Garfunkel's Greatest Hits* cassette we played constantly on that retreat, but I don't think we ever took it out of the little tape recorder someone brought along. Their music fit the moment: soft, sensitive harmonies, adolescent energy, and most of all the youthful belief in beauty—a beauty delicate, difficult to touch, but still within grasp. Simon sang of kissing honey hair with grateful tears, and I knew that gratitude was possible, and that it was *good.* I was living it, at least for a moment. At age fourteen.

Is not ingratitude a willful blindness, the mere refusal to pay attention? Is not gratitude as simple as air, as basic as blood? All that I've seen since that retreat leaves me nodding my head. . . .

An elderly Brazilian man of Italian descent stumbles from the bus stop down a long crater-filled dirt road and into our little church. If you can call it that—it's the former tribal housing of a missionary family that once worked with Indians, and is, to say the least, inelegant. The man is crippled. How he learned of us we don't know, not because he doesn't try to tell us but because we understand so little Portuguese. Despite the fact that my father, in the country only a year, has to painstakingly write out each lesson and sermon before delivering them in his heavy American, Appalachian accent, "Senhor Alfonso" comes back week after week, one of only a handful of congregants. He lights up when he hears us singing songs that sometime in his life became precious to him—mainly translations of European and American lyrics. Later he'll introduce us to his daughter and her family. They'll became a mainstay in my parents' ministry in the years that follow. . . .

I'm the R.A. on the west side of a long hall during my senior year of college, and Todd is the R.A. on the east side. It is a dorm of mainly freshmen. At the beginning of the spring semester Todd announces that he is going to begin what he calls the "Tour d'East." African-American and raised by relatives in Philadelphia, he had arrived at our white Bible college three years earlier a recent convert, "on fire," as we would say, with red t-shirts emblazoned with phrases like "Ask Me About Jesus." The fire did not die. His life during those years was a steady rebuke to me, and it remained that way to the end: Todd spends most of our last semester of college on a Pauline mission to his youthful charges, sleeping on the floor beside their bunks. . . .

When he gets word that my wife is in labor, my brother, on a lark, leaves behind his wife and three children to rush across the state in their beat-up Camry. Five hours later, as sleepy but bemused nurses look on, he gives me a bear hug. It is 3:30 a.m. He welcomes two-hour-old Christopher into the family with his typical panache and drives back home twelve hours later. The next week he calls to tell me he's still on a "high from Christopher." . . .

We're brand new to the church, but to our surprise the deacons begin a meals brigade after our third child arrives. On a hot July day a mother of an adult daughter with Williams Syndrome brings us a delicious chicken salad served in carved-out cantaloupes, along with steaming corn on the cob, which she drove over to Ohio to buy. She and her daughter run in and out of the house in a rush—they are taking a meal to another church family too, she tells me, the family of a young father dying of melanoma. . . .

A man picks up a seed and says, quietly, that unless it is buried there will be no fruit. The man later thrusts a solid, cavernous cup at his thirsty friends. Come, drink, he urges. Drink it all. Drink, and live.

Also: just before he leaves them he cooks them a breakfast of fried fish.

Just shy of twenty years after the *chapada* retreat, I'm at a fall conference on the coast of Southern California. A friend of ten years whom I met at seminary is talking to me. About gratitude. He, as much as any friend I have, knows it's a talk I need. He himself survived a bout with cancer as a teenager. He has something to say.

He talks to me about the fall, about corruption, about the curse, about our just condemnation. *Nothing* we have here, he hopes I'll grasp, is deserved. Any loss that we may sense now will be infinitely compounded if we fail to acknowledge the good that God, even as we speak, is mercifully preserving for us.

I know all of this, I think. But I also know that such knowing hasn't led to a lasting gratitude. My friend has some sense of the cramped, dank spaces I've lived in. He tries to budge the barricaded door just a crack.

A year passes, and we're at another conference. I tell him how I stood in line at the airport that morning and recalled the professor who mentored both of us during our seminary years. His faithful and wise ministrations opened my eyes to a world—or, rather, many worlds—I had never known, and showed me how I might enter them. The improbability of my pilgrimage struck me hard that morning. I realized how in many respects I had so little to do with it. It is a good confession to make: I make it to my friend, and later to my professor too.

More months pass, and finally it's spring. For the first time in my life I plant a garden. It's a tiny garden, a patch really. The soil, a thick, solid reddish clay, doomed the carrots. But the pumpkins are thriving.

It hits me, as I watch them grow, that I don't need a waterfall anymore—and not even Paul Simon. Somehow I've been made to see that the creation *is* music. Any music of our own making just helps train our ears to this other, ancient music that has been playing all the while.

It's music that emanates from a world that hangs together in Him, a world delicately calibrated, plied and pieced together with supernal care, infused with a vibrancy we cannot name but clumsily, with halting tongue.

He waits for us to name it anyway, for it is His name. Waiting, He whispers to us what He has whispered over and over from the start: Choose life, human creature, choose life. He looks down and sees that we are like grass, and that we are like sparrows, and that we are like Him. He breathes upon us, again—knowing all the while the first words we'll find ourselves saying as we awaken in that other world: *It was all a gift.* For some this will be epiphany accompanied by deepest terror. For others it will be a refrain uttered in deepest love.

It all comes down to what one makes of the blood. In terrible, beautiful fashion, it is our Creator's own blood that enables us, soiled and broken creatures that we are, to breathe this air, this fresh, clean, sweet air. Apart from this most earthy of washings, gratitude doesn't have a chance. Neither do we.

—2002

Permissions and Credits

Earlier forms of the following essays appeared in these publications.

Books & Culture: "FoodTM," May/June 2004; "The Birkenstock Brigade," May/June 2006; "Shock and Awe," September/October 2006; "The Republic of Baseball," March/April 2010.

Christian Reflection: A Series in Faith and Ethics (a publication of the Center for Christian Ethics at Baylor University): "Play On!," in volume 29 (2008).

Christianity Today: "Keeping Up with the Amish," 4 October 1999; "Broken Man" as "Aching for Something Deep," September 2003; "Why We Love Football," September 2007; "Vacationing with the Pagans" September 2009 (Web only); "Free Indeed?" as "Why We Love Amish Romances," April 2011.

The Cresset: "Wisdom for the Recovery of Local Culture," February 2003; "Centers That Hold," June 2005.

First Things: "Liberalism's Lonely Triumph" as "Alone in the Academy," February 2004.

Mars Hill Review: "Lure of the Flesh, Evasion of Flesh and Blood: Discovering the Way of Virtue," volume 21.

The New Pantagruel: "Kentucky on My Mind," Winter 2004; "Realism against Reality," Summer 2004; "Babel-On," Winter 2005.

Philadelphia Inquirer: "In Search of Faces, Books, and Friends" as "Face It: 'Friends' Aren't," 8 September 2009.

Touchstone: "Elusive Unity," April 2005.

Lyrics by Mark Heard are quoted from Matthew Dickerson, *Hammers and Nails: The Life and Music of Mark Heard* (Chicago: Cornerstone, 2003).